Time Management

FOR BUSY PEOPLE

Roberta Roesch

McGraw-Hill

New York   San Francisco   Washington D.C.   Auckland   Bogotá
Caracas   Lisbon   London   Madrid   Mexico City   Milan
Montreal   New Delhi   San Juan   Singapore
Sydney   Tokyo   Toronto

Library of Congress Catalog Card Number: 98-65522

McGraw-Hill

A Division of The McGraw·Hill Companies

1 2 3 4 5 6 7 8 9 0 DOC/DOC 9 0 3 2 1 0 9 8

ISBN 0-07-053406-3 (pbk.)

*The sponsoring editor for this book was Susan Barry, the assistant editor
was Griffin Hansbury, the editing supervisor was Christina Palaia, and
the production supervisor was Tina Cameron. It was set in Adobe
Garamond by North Market Street Graphics.*

Printed and bound by R. R. Donnelley & Sons Company.

McGraw-Hill books are available at special quantity discounts to use
as premiums and sales promotions, or for use in corporate training
sessions. For more information, please write to the Director of Special
Sales, McGraw-Hill, 11 West 19th Street, New York, NY 10011. Or
contact your local bookstore.

CONTENTS

9 Flex Your Time: Working from Home and Other Options — 153

10   Simplify and Equalize: Home, Family, and Nonwork Time   177

11   Minimize *Must* Home Chores Time, Maximize *Should, Want, and Soul-Searching* Time   197

ACKNOWLEDGMENTS
Many people have a part in the making of all books and the same is true of this one. Though most of the experiences and observations come from my life and work a wide variety of other people shared expertise, too.

Those who contributed tips for the last chapter are mentioned at the end of that chapter. Others who helped get this book on track are Stephanie Denton, Debbie Gilster, Jann Jasper, Donna McMillan, Alison Berke, Franklynn Peterson, Terri Lonier, Marya Charles Alexander, Jim Saelzler, Michael Marcus, Marilyn Miglin, Johanna Garaventa, Dan Nesbett, Dr. Robert J. Wicks, Dr. Donald R. Gallagher, Sunny Schlenger, Enterprise Rent-A-Car, TravRoute Software, and Courtyard By Marriott. A major thank you goes to my editors Susan Barry and Griffin Hansbury, my agent Bert Holtje, and my computer consultant Terry Good.

No thanks and words of appreciation would be complete without my ongoing gratitude to my family—my husband Phil, my son Jeff who pitched in with his culinary skills to give me extra time on this book, and my daughter Meredith who was always there with ideas and encouragement. I give special thanks to my editor-daughter Bonnie Roesch whose editing, professional assistance, and generosity with her time saved me many hours in moving this book to completion. Thank you all.
Roberta Roesch

INTRODUCTION

If you're a busy person who believes "I don't have time to read time books," *this book is for you!*

I wrote it because I know how much you need and want a *quick* read that will fit your busy lifestyle with its ever expanding demands on your time.

I know how busy you are. Because we all have many roles, time management today doesn't stand alone. Instead it includes life and self-management—and the values that are important in the way we use our time. Increasingly, people are paying greater attention to this, so this book—with its *streamlined* reading—focuses on this harmonious whole. You'll find it isn't a "rules" book with instructions set in stone. Rather it's a guide to a *personal* approach to managing your time, life, and self in a way that will give you what you need in all the roles you play.

Naturally, the classic time management tools continue to be an important part of our lives, so they're given just due in this book. For a fast refresher on them, start by reading each chapter—and its introduction—quickly to get an overall view of what will be most helpful to you in developing a quick-action and *workable* time management plan. Then, before going to the next chapter, reread each one thoroughly and stop frequently to think about how to apply to your life the quick and concise ideas for surviving the daily time crunch and accomplishing what you need and want to do.

A Guide to Using This Book

You can use this book as a reference, or you can read it from cover to cover. Here's a quick rundown of the important elements you'll find as you go along:

Fast Forwards

Each chapter begins with a section called Fast Forward. They will offer you everything you need to know in one quick bite—sort of the *Reader's Digest* version of the chapter. Each one is a nifty little illustrated reference guide that summarizes the key points found in the chapter.

To make things easier, each one will include page references to guide you to more complete explanations later in the chapter.

Habits & Strategies

These notes convey timesaving tips that appear as reader-friendly highlighted boxes throughout the text. Even if you're already a time-crunching expert, don't overlook these quick tips, techniques, and tidbits. They'll give you the big picture and help you plan ahead.

Minutes Matter

These brief tips will be sprinkled throughout the book as quick ways to get the most out of every minute.

Cautions

There's a right way and a wrong way to do most things in life. These brief notes alert you to the dangers of procrastination, trying to be a perfectionist, taking on too many tasks, and other time management pitfalls.

STEP BY STEP

Step-by-Steps

Many of the tips in this book really need detailed instructions to carry out. You'll easily be able to recognize these step-by-step boxes where you can find these details.

Checkpoints

At the end of each chapter, you'll get a summary of important points from the previous chapter and a preview of what's coming in the next chapter.

Let's Go!

As this *quick* read becomes your personal handbook on the way you manage your time, life, and self, you'll discover you *can* find the time you need for the multiple roles you fill. You'll be able to invest your hours in what you value most.

Start *Now*—Make Today Your *First Day*

INCLUDES

- First day steps for launching a better time-managed life
- Taking an objective look at what you accomplish—and don't accomplish—in your workday
- Beginning your day
- Getting a handle on what must be done and what should be done
- Establishing doable goals for the musts and shoulds
- Allotting time for these tasks and commitments
- Reacting to interruptions
- Charting your time as you work
- Ending the first day

FAST FORWARD

Begin Today ➤ *pp. 6–7*

- Take a pencil and paper and list what you *do* and *don't* have time for in your work life and home, family, and personal life.
- Assess where you stand and what you need to change.

Wake-up Call ➤ *pp. 7–8*

- Set two alarm clocks.
- Put both away from your bed so you have to rise to turn them off.
- Stay up.
- Think of positive, rather than negative, upcoming things for the day.

Arrive at Work on Time ➤ *pp. 8–9*

- Reach your desk before the phones ring and people drop in.
- Spend a few minutes putting information you'll need for incoming and outgoing phone calls by your phone so you won't waste time on a hunting trip when it's time for the calls.
- Avoid procrastinating on important things by succumbing to the all-too-human habit of doing warm-up and not-getting-going jobs first.
- Begin work immediately on what you've designated as your number 1 task for the day.

Set Up Realistic Goals ➤ *pp. 9–10*

- Think beyond number 1 goal to the other tasks and commitments on your mind and agenda.
- Evaluate the importance of each and decide which to do next in 2, 3, and 4 order.
- Know the difference between *ideal* and *possible* and be practical about *overplanning* so you won't experience a "nothing done" frustration at the end of the day.

Use Lists, Appointment Books, and Calendars ➤ *pp. 10–11*

- Make your lists as simple as possible so they won't look overwhelming.
- Decide whether a computerized contact manager that puts your to-do list, appointment book, and calendar inside your computer; a commercial planner/organizer; or a self-created planner and to-do form will work best for you.
- While listing your top and middle concerns, note the lower-ranking jobs you've been postponing but would like to get done when you find time. Whenever you have unexpected spare minutes, choose one of the tasks and tackle small portions of it.

Estimate Time Frames ➤ *pp. 12–13*

- Figure out how much time each of your day's tasks and commitments should take—and add a little extra time. Match that estimate to the workday time you have and coordinate the two.
- Keep your eye on that time frame as you work and push yourself to stay within it as well as you can. Accept the fact that for many jobs it's more important to pace yourself to turn in a *possible good* job on time than to hold back on deadlines while you strive for the *ideal perfect* job.

Resist Interruptions ➤ *pp. 13–15*

- Establish times when you make or take phone calls.
- Use voice mail or an answering machine to screen calls and help you cut down on calls you don't need or want to take.
- Read and reply to e-mail and fax messages all at one time.
- Tell people it's not a good time for you to talk when they interrupt you with matters that aren't urgent.

Track Where the Minutes and Hours Go ➤ *pp. 15–17*

- As you proceed through your first day, maintain a log of exactly what you do and how long you spend doing it.
- Compare this to the projections you made when you blocked out your tasks and estimated amount of time they'd take.
- Use this comparison to get a handle on reality.

Blueprint Your Next Day's Timetable ➤ *p. 17*

- Prepare for a good start on your next day by checking that day's calendar and appointment book before leaving work.
- Decide on the 1-2-3-4 order of important tasks to be done.
- Plan for meetings, conferences, appointments, and lunches.
- Do a quick rough draft of your next day's timetable.

Celebrate Making It Through Your First Day ➤ *p. 18*

- Give yourself a pat on the back for accomplishing the *possible*.
- Take a quiz to evaluate how you feel about your first day.
- Refuse to feel guilty if you didn't stay entirely on schedule and check off all your to-dos.

Be Kind to Yourself While New Habits Kick In ➤ *p. 19*

- Time management takes time.
- Be patient and concentrate on improving yours one day at a time.

The clock ticks. The minutes fly. And in your high-speed life, your days seem like an endless race to catch a rapidly moving train that's pulling out of the station and leaving you behind.

We've all had this sense of missing time trains and being left behind, when, in addition to our work, we're faced with demands in our other roles—in families, home, community, and by friends, to say nothing of our personal lives.

I've reported on people's struggle with time for over 25 years and, in talking to thousands from all walks of life, I've found the busiest persons—in the toughest time binds—*can* learn to get on the right time track through streamlining the basic time management rules, matching the time-tested fundamentals to their personal no-time-to-lose approach, and living by minutes matter strategies as minutes add up to the hours that become the days of our lives.

Would *Your* Schedule Make Strong Men and Women Cry?

The time-tested truths for managing time have never really changed, and the basics continue to hold their own as turn-of-the-century classics. And no matter how beat and busy you are,

There are ways to streamline the basics and make both your time and life management work.

There are ways to draw on your time reserves and tame your time management demons.

This chapter will give you start-up streamliners and first-day steps for accomplishing what you need and want to do. Then, subsequent chapters follow up on the first-day steps, so you can take weekly and monthly strides to make your work and multiple roles less complicated, convoluted, and complex.

Begin Today—Not Someday

"Today is the time when something gets done, or not done; it can't be yesterday, and there are no guarantees about tomorrow."
Alec Mackenzie, consultant, Alex Mackenzie's Time Tactics

No, you're not too busy to make today the *first* day of your upgraded time-managed life. In fact, there's no better time than the present to get an upper hand on time and begin to take increased control of your work and life. So, get out your pencil and paper because, if you're like most of us, the list of what you want to do, never have time to do, and *really* want to have time for is probably as lengthy as train tracks from New York to California.

Here's Where Lists Come In

This chapter admittedly is *lists à la mode,* but these are lists that *work.* Bear with me and believe that even though making a list takes time, *some* are fun and revealing and worth the time they take.

Here are your lists for starters. Use all the lines you need.

STEP BY STEP

Lists

The Things I *Do* Have Time For

Work Life   *Home/Family/Personal Life*

_____   _____
_____   _____
_____   _____
_____   _____
_____   _____

The Things I *Don't* Have Time For

Work Life   *Home/Family/Personal Life*

_____   _____
_____   _____
_____   _____
_____   _____

> **The Things I *Really* Want Time For**
>
> ***Work Life***   ***Home/Family/Personal Life***
>
> _____   _____
>
> _____   _____
>
> _____   _____
>
> _____   _____

As you evaluate your lists, you'll see at a glance that you *usually* find time for the things you enjoy, not for some things you *really* want time for, and *certainly* not for what you don't want to do or don't want to do enough.

That's human! So, hang on to your lists. We'll return to them later. Then, by the time you finish this book, you'll definitely have better control of the things you have time for, the things you don't have time for, and the things you really want time for.

Wake Up to a First Day Upper Rather than a Downer

How you get moving in the morning can affect your entire day, so opt for an upbeat wake-up call rather than a downbeat one.

The Downbeat Wake-up Call

How common it is to awaken thinking about the memo that upset you yesterday, or the dental appointment for root canal that's ahead for today. Either is sufficiently negative to make you want to cover your head and delay getting out of bed.

The Upbeat Wake-up Call

A far better way to start your first day of making your time and life management work is to block out your anxieties and think, instead, of three upcoming things that will give you pleasure. They don't have to be as major as winning the lottery. Be realistic, like the account manager who gets herself up and running by thinking of

1. French-roast coffee and a hot cinnamon bun for breakfast

2. Listening to a new Celine Dion tape while going to work

3. Bowling later that night

After turning off the alarm—or during your shower-dressing routine—follow her example and look forward to three small pleasures that, throughout the day, will enhance your sense of well-being. As simple as this probably sounds, it's an upper for getting started.

HABITS & STRATEGIES

Make sure you get up when you plan to by setting two alarms. Put both clocks across the room out of reach so you have to get out of bed to turn them off. Then stay up. This may be one of the hardest things you have to do all day, but it pays time dividends.

Arrive at Work on Time— Or Before Time

You'll be less harried and hurried all day if you get to your desk *before* the phones ring and *before* other people interrupt you. When you get there on time or before time,

Do

1. Decide on your most essential first-things-first task for the day and place everything relating to that in the most prominent spot on your desk.

2. Prepare for important incoming and outgoing phone calls by putting together all the information you'll need for those calls.

3. Set up similar plan-aheads for meetings, conferences, and appointments

Don't

1. Procrastinate by sharpening pencils, shuffling papers, and doing non-getting-going jobs

2. Give in to the temptation to check your e-mail first and read and reply to that at once

3. Make an early-morning phone call that doesn't have to be made

CAUTION

If you're late to work, you hit red lights before you get anywhere. You then spend the entire working day trying to make the green lights.

Set Up Realistic Work Goals

You've already pinpointed your number 1 job—your main goal for the day. Now look at the following:

- The two, three, four, and five other tasks and commitments you must or should attend to
- Scheduled appointments inside and outside of the office
- Meetings
- Jobs you're constantly reminded of that you've been putting off

Instead of feeling overwhelmed by all you have to do, reevaluate the foregoing and make a firm decision about which tasks you will follow through. Most people tend to overplan (that's one of our time management demons). Try to be objective about the time your tasks will take and the number of hours you actually have to work on each of them.

MINUTES MATTER

Recognize the inconsequential and ignore it.

There's seldom a day when any of us gets to everything, so sidestep that "nothing done" frustration at the end of the day by determining whether all the tasks, commitments, meetings, and appointments you are looking at *have* to be taken care of that day.

Know the difference between *ideal* and *possible* and drop nonessential items so you won't be overwhelmed. Maybe—with your tongue in cheek—you'll even want to consider a *not-to-do-today* list!

In a more serious vein, however, *do* choose a to-do list instead.

HABITS & STRATEGIES

When you decide what tasks to do, ask the person who has final approval on that work any questions you have so you won't waste time doing the work incorrectly.

Use Lists, Appointment Books, and Calendars to Put Your Plans into Action

Though some people balk at making lists, lists *still* get a number 10 rating for helping you get what you want to get done—*if* you keep your lists simple. This applies whether you use

- A computerized contact manager that puts your to-do list, appointment book, and calendar inside your computer
- A commercial day planner or calendar
- An uncomplicated step-by-step to-do form you create for yourself

"Think of making lists as a way of expanding your own memory capacity."
Sheree Bykofsky, author of *500 Terrific Ideas for Organizing Everything*

I love my computer dearly—and I couldn't work without it. But, still, when it comes to making lists, I'm an all-out booster for the step-by-step form I've created for myself. It works, and it's as simple as this:

Whether you choose to plan your day with a computer contact manager, commercial day planner, or self-created form, begin your to-dos by putting under

STEP BY STEP

Day Plan

**What Must Be Done and
Must Appointments
and Meetings**

**What Should Be Done and
Possible Appointments
and Meetings**

**What Would Be Good to Get Done
and Future Appointments and Meetings**

What *Must* Be Done your essential first-things-first number 1 goal plus one or two of the two, three, four, or five other tasks or commitments you must or should attend to. Put the others under What Should Be Done.

Under What Would Be Good to Get Done, list (1) things you don't want to forget; (2) tasks of lower value that you'd like to get done; and (3) jobs you've been postponing. Whenever you have unexpected spare time, tackle one of the latter categories.

Estimate Time Frames for Must-Be-Dones and Should-Be-Dones

Since it *is* a human frailty to overplan and be unrealistic about how long a task will take versus how much time you have to do it, make a conscious effort to (1) estimate in advance how much working time you'll need to do a *good* job (all jobs don't have to be *perfect*) on each task or commitment, and (2) determine when you can designate blocks of time to take care of each.

MINUTES MATTER

Avoid the perfectionist trap. In many situations, it's more important to strive for a good *job that you can hand in on time rather than a* perfect *job you're never ready to deliver.*

In an eight-hour work day, count on six to seven hours of solid working time for what-must-be-dones and what-should-be-dones. Then, over and above your lunch break, plan for one hour of open time for the unavoidable matters that pop in and out of your day.

HABITS & STRATEGIES

When you list your to-dos make a mental note to be flexible, adaptable, and spontaneous when the need or mood arises. No lists are so set in concrete you're chained to a slab of stone.

Block Out Time Slots for Your Day's Agenda on Your Calendar and in Your Appointment Book

Once you've matched your tasks and commitments to your time estimates, write the tasks and time blocks on your calendar—your computer calendar, if that's your choice, or your standard calendar, if you prefer that. Whatever your choice,

- Put your calendar/appointment book in your carry-all to bring from home to office and vice versa
- Keep it on your desk while at work
- Take it to meetings and appointments

There are many views on whether to use one or multiple calendars. My choice is definitely *one* calendar (after trying multiple ones). But, be absolutely sure to coordinate your calendar and appointment book daily so you mark everything on both.

HABITS & STRATEGIES

Write addresses and phone numbers by the names of persons with whom you have appointments so you can contact them quickly for confirmations and changes of plans. In your appointment book and calendar, use the top of each space allotted for each day for work plans and appointments and the bottom for home and personal commitments. Use colored pencils—one color for work, another for home and personal.

Resist the Temptation to React to Interruptions

A frequent time demon that holds you from moving ahead with your plans is the habit of responding too quickly to (1) phone calls, (2) faxes, e-mail, and the day's mail, and (3) staff questions and drop-in visits. Here are time-savers for combatting these deterrents:

Phone Calls

- Establish times when you make or take phone calls—say, before lunch or at the end of the day. Then, as much as possible, ignore the phone completely when you're involved in more important have-to-get-finished work.

- Eliminate as many calls as you can by using voice mail or an answering machine to record messages, screen calls, and help cut down on calls you don't need or want to take.
- As you listen to your messages, consolidate them. In your time slot for making calls, respond only to those that require a reply. As much as possible, try to do all the callbacks at one time. Even with the busy, on holds, and not availables you inevitably get on some, you'll still spend a shorter time on the phone—and it will be on *your* time schedule instead of an interruption later.
- When you make or take your calls, master the art of ending conversations quickly and graciously.

MINUTES MATTER

Spare yourself from having to listen to long-winded incoming messages on your answering machine by saying in your taped message "You have 90 seconds to leave a message."

Faxes, E-mail, and the Day's Mail

- Read and reply to e-mail and fax messages all at one time rather than message by message.
- When the day's mail arrives, discipline yourself to scan it quickly so it won't disrupt what you're doing for too long. During your quick scan, use a highlighting pen to mark important items. This will save time when you handle the mail later on.
- If you *must* do more than scan your mail, sort it quickly into five categories: for immediate response; to go over later; to read more thoroughly; to file; to throw out. Use the wastebasket to file the latter *at once.*

Staff Questions and Drop-in Visits

Despite the need to resist interruptions, we all encounter people interruptions, and there's no way to eliminate this entirely. There are *always* some situations when people must come ahead of your plans. After all, you're paid to respond to interruptions from your boss—and customers and clients.

But you're not paid to lose time from your work simply to pass the time of day with coworkers who are taking a break or persons who want to discuss their problems or ask for information that could wait until another time. To minimize these interruptions,

- Give people to whom you delegate work full instructions on how you want things done so they won't have to break into your day with requests for further information
- Train people to save up necessary questions so you can provide answers all at one time rather than piecemeal
- Say, "This isn't a good time for me to talk" when you're interrupted with a matter that isn't urgent
- Put a sign on your door or the wall outside your cubicle saying, "I'm not available until P.M. Please do not disturb."

HABITS & STRATEGIES

When you allow unnecessary interruptions, they take a toll on your time and put you in a catch-up position for the rest of the day. Cut down on the nonessential interruptions by establishing regular times when people can come to you for answers to unforeseen problems and questions. Simultaneously, make it clear that there are regular times when you're not available. When people don't respect this, respond with "Later, not now."

Track Where the Minutes and Hours Go

Now that you've set up first-day plans and know what must and should be done, keep a daily time log for this first day and note exactly what you do and how long you spend doing it. Include your time spent at lunch and coffee breaks. You'll discover where your time is going—or where it isn't going. You'll get a handle on reality and spot diversions that waste your time.

As a simpler and faster alternative to the traditional time log that lists your hour-by-hour activities, make a pie chart for your workday. (See diagram for pie-chart circles for morning and afternoon.) Make similar charts for your day and fill in the segments as you proceed through the day.

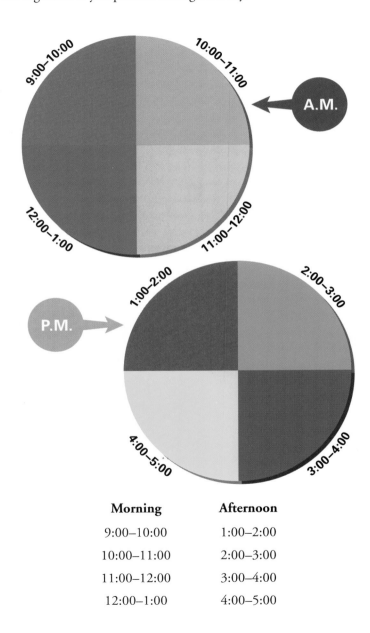

Morning	Afternoon
9:00–10:00	1:00–2:00
10:00–11:00	2:00–3:00
11:00–12:00	3:00–4:00
12:00–1:00	4:00–5:00

Write all your activities on the charts (including wasted time). Then as you evaluate your filled-in segments, underline in red the time wasters you could have eliminated to get more of what you needed and wanted to get done.

Blueprint Your Next Day's Timetable

Close the first day of your upgraded time-managed life by taking a few minutes at the end of the day to put away papers and clear your desk. Then check your next day's calendar and appointment book and make a working list of your must-be-dones and should-be-dones. Do what you did for your first day and write beside each task the estimated time each will or should take.

As noted earlier in this chapter, on your first day of improving your time and life management, you'll take time at the *beginning* of that first morning to (1) decide on your most essential first-things-first tasks, (2) plan for meetings, conferences, and appointments, and (3) set up minutes or hours to handle incoming and outgoing messages and phone calls.

After that first day, however, you'll be doing this at the *end* of the day. This will avoid wasting time in the morning while you decide what to do. Here's how an art director on a food magazine rough-drafted his next day's timetable.

"When meeting with busy people ask for the first appointment of the day. Your chances of having to wait are reduced."
Odette Pollar, management and organization consultant

- Meet with editor first thing in morning to discuss illustrations for articles planned for Christmas issue—1 hour
- Go over and make necessary changes on layout for pasta recipe piece for upcoming issue—½ hour
- Interview three job applicants for assistant art director's opening—(½ hour each) 1½ hours
- Have lunch with Ed to discuss photo possibilities for January cover—1½ hours
- Attend afternoon staff meeting—1½ hours
- Get e-mail and voice mail messages and reply—1 hour
- Open time for emergencies and catch up—1 hour

Celebrate Making It through Your First Day

At the end of your first workday on your upgraded time management regime, take this yes or no questionnaire and check the appropriate spaces.

First Day Checkup Questionnaire

	Yes	No
1. Did you make a conscious effort when you woke up to think of three upcoming things that would give you pleasure throughout the day?	—	—
2. Did you or will you still do those things today?	—	—
3. Did you get to work on time?	—	—
4. Did you accomplish at least a fair portion of your Must-Dos and Should-Dos?	—	—
5. Even if you didn't get everything done, do you feel less of the nothing-done frustration you sometimes experience?	—	—
6. Did you follow through on the suggested lists à la mode rather than skimming over them?	—	—
7. Did you coordinate your calendar/appointment book so that at all times you knew what you were supposed to do and when and where you were supposed to be doing it?	—	—
8. Did you manage to cut down on some interruptions?	—	—
9. Did you use the pie charts to track your time and note exactly what you did and how long you spent doing it?	—	—
10. Do you have a working blueprint of your agenda for tomorrow?	—	—
Total	—	—

If your total yes answers outweigh the nos, you have cause to celebrate. But, regardless of what your total is, give yourself a pat on the back for accomplishing the possible. Don't feel guilty this first day if you didn't stay entirely on schedule and check off all your to-dos. This goes with the territory called life in even the best time management plans.

Be Kind to Yourself While New Habits Kick In

"Our two greatest gifts are time and the freedom to choose—the power to direct our efforts in the use of that time."
Stephen R. Covey, founder of Covey Leadership Center

As you progress from your first day to managing your weeks—and later, months—concentrate on improving your time management one day at a time. While you develop your own special strengths, begin with small steps and give yourself time to upgrade your performance. If one day falls apart for one reason or another, roll with the punches and get a new start on the following day. *Don't* let frustration take over and push you back to your old ways.

Instead, be patient with yourself and know that managing time *takes* time. But, like other busy people, you can learn—sooner than you think—to streamline the fundamentals and match the time-tested basics to your no-time-to-lose approach.

Checkpoints

You have learned how to take first-day steps to put time on your side.

You have taken an objective look at what you have time for, what you don't have time for, and what you *really* want to have time for.

You have observed how much time your daily goals should and do take and have come to terms with matching those goals to the time you have.

You have determined how to avoid interruptions and the nothing-done frustration at the end of the workday.

In the next chapter, you will see how to progress from your first day start-up to a weekly time management system.

CHAPTER

2

Get a Fix on Your Time One Week at a Time

INCLUDES

- Setting an action plan
- Learning to valutize
- Scheduling your week
- Keeping a weekly log
- Reevaluating and moving on

FAST FORWARD

Plan Your Week ➤ *pp. 24–28*

- Make a preliminary assessment, in writing, of your goals for the week and the actions needed to accomplish them.
- *Valutize* your list by assessing a value and degree of importance to what you need and want to do.
- Allow for flexibility in your appraisals, assigning new values to activities when unforeseen problems arise or new responsibilities are introduced.
- Create a weekly *master-list plan* based on your valutized list, including immediate action items, projects needing completion by week's end, and new tasks to be initiated.
- Attach a time estimate to each activity on your master-list plan.

Schedule ➤ *pp. 28–31*

- Employ a variety of tactics—such as breaking up objectives into small steps or checking off completed actions—as a way to optimize the use of your schedule.
- Transfer your weekly goals from your *master-list plan* to your calendar, *evenly* distributing the work over five days.
- Ensure that your organizing calendar is your *all-purpose* and *only* calendar for both work and personal commitments.
- Add a scribble pad to your planner for jotting down notes and ideas that you can access quickly.

Weekly Log ➤ *pp. 31–35*

- Keep a weekly log that includes everything on your *master-list plan,* noting your previously estimated time as well as your actual time needed to complete each task.
- Pinpoint loopholes in your days that nibble away at your time and energy and prevent you from concentrating on more significant obligations.

- Compare actual time spent to projected time and use this knowledge to formulate a more effective blueprint in the coming weeks.

Moving On ➤ *pp. 35–36*

- Evaluate the helpfulness of your weekly log at the week's end.
- Reevaluate and revise those parts of the log that weren't effective for you.
- Be patient—reminding yourself that getting the *right* things done is more important than getting everything done.

Your time is your life—and the *present* is what you have this week—so, just as you boarded the time train for a first day "no time to lose" trip, continue down the tracks to a one-week journey committed to expanding Chap. 1's streamlining basics. Some people find that weekly planning works best in their situations, so they integrate and expand the daily streamlines that, together, make a week's whole. This approach for handling your workweek can help you achieve a big time payoff.

Weekly Timetable
Mon. to Fri. = 120 hours
Sat. and Sun. = 48 hours
Weekly Total = 168 hours

On your way to this time-saving payoff, however, keep in mind that no one *ever* uses *every* streamliner, so adapt the ones that reduce *your* time squeeze and fit *your* work and life. *Remember: There's* never *just* one *way to manage time!*

Make a Plan for Your Week

Admittedly, planning what you need to do takes both time and thought. But the end results maximize your time, so copy and fill in the following questionnaire to get a clear view of an action plan for the coming week.

HABITS & STRATEGIES

Know what you need to accomplish in a week, but don't start out to beat the world. Be realistic about what you can actually do and avoid the no-win situation of trying to know, do, and be everything in your 168 hours.

Take This Weekly Planning Questionnaire

What do I want done by Friday? _____

What steps do I have to take to do this? _____

What tasks must I do in segments each day to meet the Friday goal? _____

Roughly, how much time will each daily task take? _____

How does what I want to get done this week complement what I want from my work and life? _____

What can I eliminate that doesn't supplement that? _____

Set Up and Valutize Your Week's Objectives

Instead of the tired *prioritize* we've all heard over and over, we're updating the word to *valutize*—assigning a value and degree of importance to what you need and want to do—in the pages of this book. To valutize,

- Determine what is most essential and important to get done during the week using the weekly master-list plan on page 26.
- Assess all the activities you list to see if all the tasks and projects really must be done.
- Ruthlessly weed out or cut back on unnecessary tasks that don't contribute to what you need or want to accomplish.
- Review the activities that remain and identify the specific actions you need to take to get moving on them.
- Take the *right* action and bear in mind you'll be wasting your time and energy whenever you fall back into the trap of spending these two invaluables on tasks you ruled out instead of spending them on the larger, more significant things that would provide real purpose and payoff.

"Webster's definition of a colander: A perforated pan for draining liquids. My definition: An object with holes in it to drain out what is not necessary and to save what is."
Karen Okulicz, author of Try!

- Expect that your valutizing may change throughout the week, depending on circumstances (e.g., crises, teamwork plans, and unpredictable matters that are beyond your control). Be prepared for some crisis management and adjustments to your plans when bona fide situations arise.
- Assign a value to new tasks as they come up during the week.
- Know your limits and be practical about how much you can really expect to get done.

HABITS & STRATEGIES

The need to shift gears is a fact of life in everybody's week, so accept necessary changes and the need to revise your plans. That's part of getting a fix on your time and performing effectively.

Prepare Your Weekly Master-List Plan

I can hear you say, "Not another list—that means more paperwork!" But the proven benefit of on-paper lists (or electronic lists) is the way they provide hands-on control and save time in the long haul.

After your valutizing session, make copies of the following form so you have a supply for several weeks. Then, just as you made a day plan in Chap. 1, make a weekly master-list plan. Use legal size paper for your copies since this size will hold the full form. The margins will give you backup room for changes or additional items you may need to insert during the week. Fill in the blanks with pencil since even the best weekly planning sometimes requires reordering.

Step-by-Step Weekly Master-List Plan
For Immediate Action:

_____

_____

Estimated time this will take: _____

Dates due: _____

To Finish by End of Week:

_____

_____

   Estimated time this will take: _____

   Dates due: _____

Down-the-Track Projects to Get Started On:

_____

_____

   Estimated time this will take: _____

   Dates due: _____

People to Contact:

_____

_____

   Estimated time this will take: _____

Meetings and Appointments:

_____

_____

   Estimated time this will take: _____

Important Phone Calls to Make:

_____

_____

   Estimated time this will take: _____

Routine Tasks and Paperwork:

_____

_____

   Estimated time this will take: _____

   Dates due: _____

On-Hold Nonurgents (Would be nice, but not necessary now):

_____

_____

   (No time estimate since this is arbitrary)

CAUTION

Keep your planning sheets simple.

MINUTES MATTER

Avoid repeating tasks too often.

Now that you know where you're going for the week, a schedule will help you get there.

Schedule Your Week

Know when to blow the whistle on planning and start scheduling.

Schedules are the engines that make *master-list plans* work, so planning that's not followed by scheduling is a one-way ticket to nowhere. An electronic or on-paper schedule, however, sidetracks this unwelcome deadend because you can

See at a glance what you have to do, and then concentrate fully on doing it

Cut down on wasting time worrying about how to get everything done

Save time by not having to rewrite your schedule every day

Six Scheduling Optimizers

1. Break up your larger weekly objectives into smaller Monday-to-Friday increments. Plan on doing the most essential ones at the best time of day for you to get things done.

2. Avoid overscheduling. For a less stressful week, leave some time cushions for breaks, breathers, crises, emergencies, and catching up.

3. Review your schedule throughout the day.

4. During the week, check off each objective as you complete it. The good feeling you experience will inspire you to keep moving ahead.

5. Check the following day's schedule before leaving work and shift your still-to-do tasks to the next day as necessary.

6. Accept the reality that you can't always expect to cross off all of the tasks on your weekly plan at the end of the week.

CAUTION

Don't let list-making time take the place of doing-time. Lists are made to be carried out.

Schedule Your Week's Activities Evenly

So you won't weigh down any one day, transfer the objectives on your *master-list plan* evenly to a computerized contact manager (see Chap. 5), commercial planner/organizer, or self-created planner. Choose the method that works best for you, but your choice must integrate the projects on your *master-list plan,* your agenda for working on those projects, your meetings and appointments, your paperwork, and your important phone calls to make. As an extra plus, keep a scribble pad to record the miscellany that comes up every day.

As you did for your weekly master-list plan, use a pencil for your scheduling since few schedules work out exactly as planned. Generally, you'll find that by Wednesday you'll need to erase and refocus a plan that, on Monday or Tuesday, sounded great for midweek.

MINUTES MATTER

Don't waste your time on "trash" jobs. Get to the work that will highlight your productivity.

Commercial Planners/Organizers

An ideal planner/organizer, which can be as elaborate or simple as you wish, is one that's approximately 8 × 10—a size that will let you keep a scribble pad clipped to the front or back of it. The planner/organizer will help you coordinate your activities and provides a section for names, addresses, and phone numbers.

A calendar is a vital part of your planner/organizer. You'll want a yearly calendar that provides week-by-week pages. The safest way to make absolutely sure your calendar is foolproof is to have your planner/organizer calendar be your all-purpose calendar and the *only* one you use for your work and personal commitments. The 8 × 10 planner size is a space-saver on your desk and an easy fit for a briefcase, carry-all, or purse when you're away from your desk.

Write down on your weekly calendar all work and personal activities as well as any trips to be made. Mark anything especially important with a neon-colored highlighter.

Self-created Scheduling Plans

I'm an advocate of this choice, supplemented by my scribble pad. Thus, the planner I swear by is a loose-leaf notebook that's the size of my 6 × 9 scribble pad. It has pockets in the front and back covers and differently colored paper for each section I've set up.

At the front of the notebook, in valutized order, I allocate one section to each project I'm working on. I note the date each project should be done and write down the days I plan to work on it. I shift pages around as necessary, and when a project or job is completed, I either dispose of the page or file it if I want it for a permanent record.

Another section (and another colored paper) is reserved for the week's meetings and appointments while a third section (and a third color) is for reminders about paperwork, phone calls, and people to contact. At the back of the notebook, I keep notations about ongoing down-the-track projects and things on hold.

The pockets at the front and back of the book are important because I tuck my one and only calendar—a 5½ × 3½ week-by-week calendar—in the front pocket and my scribble pad in the back pocket. This self-created planner works for me. It's simple and without extraneous things I don't want to be bothered with.

A travel agent who uses a similar self-created plan depends on 3 × 5 index cards instead of notebook sections. There is one card for each project listing its due date and the time frame for working on it. Other cards (one for each category) detail (1) weekly meetings, (2) appointments, (3) paperwork, (4) phone calls to make with the accompanying phone numbers, (5) people to contact, including reminders of why she's contacting them, and (6) future plans with projected dates attached.

She arranges the cards in the order in which tasks should be done, holds them together with an elastic band, and rearranges as the need arises. She carries them in a see-through plastic pencil case that also holds a small week-by-week calendar and a similarly small address book.

HABITS & STRATEGIES

Have these items with you at all times:

Your commercial planner/organizer or your self-created plan
(so you can replan, reschedule, or cancel at a minute's notice)
Your scribble pad
Important addresses and phone numbers
Your business cards

Scribble Pads

Although most commercial planners have notebooks for jotting down information and miscellaneous material, there's nothing like a special scribble pad attached to the front or back of your planning device. I've just passed my silver anniversary of using pad after pad, and this mixed bag of assorted information is a quick-action reference guide that saves chunks of time. A 6 × 9 steno pad works well for writing lists, notes, ideas, inspirations, purchases, facts and figures, and other vital things. If you date a page or group of pages for each day of the week, you can have easy access to information that often gets lost in the cracks. When my current scribble pad is filled, I keep it at least two years. A library director has a three-year collection of every detail he needs to remember about a building program.

Keep a Weekly Log

Just as you kept a daily time log for your first day plans in Chap. 1, chart your time in a weekly log—what you do and how long you spend doing it. This time around, however, use the following log rather than the pie-chart circles suggested in Chap. 1.

"Studies on human concentration show that it rises and falls in 90-minutes cycles. Every hour and a half take a break for at least 10 minutes so your capacity for work can be restored."
Marcia Yudkin, consultant and publisher

A weekly log will benefit you in the following ways:

- It shows you what you're doing from one day to the next.
- It helps you get a better fix on your weekly time investment by displaying specifically exactly how much time each activity *actually* takes.
- It gives you a whole new view of how to continue to improve your time management by pinpointing loopholes in your expenditure of time in which (despite your weekly master-list plan) minutes and hours are slipping away during your 168 hours each week.

Some people shy away from logs because they see them as a time cost rather than an investment.

"That was my feeling," an engineer admits. "But once I invested the initial time and formed the habit of logging my time it paid real dividends. In the beginning I was discouraged by the whole procedure when I saw how much time I lost in bits and pieces. But as I continue keeping the log it definitely helps me use my time better."

The log that follows will help you compare your actual time spent on tasks to the projections you made when you blocked out your weekly objectives and estimated the amount of time they'd take. Make multiple copies of the log because once you have copies and follow through weekly, you'll escalate your time for subsequent weeks. Use all the lines you need when you set up your own log.

Immediate Action Jobs	Est. Time	Actual Time
Mon.		
Tues.		
Wed.		
Thurs.		
Fri.		

Finish by End of Week Jobs	**Est. Time**	**Actual Time**
Mon.		
Tues.		
Wed.		
Thurs.		
Fri.		

Down the Track Projects	**Est. Time**	**Actual Time**
Mon.		
Tues.		
Wed.		
Thurs.		
Fri.		

People Contacted & Important Phone Calls Made	**Est. Time**	**Actual Time**
Mon.		
Tues.		
Wed.		
Thurs.		
Fri.		

Meetings & Appointments	Est. Time	Actual Time
Mon.		
Tues.		
Wed.		
Thurs.		
Fri.		

Routine Tasks & Paperwork	Est. Time	Actual Time
Mon.		
Tues.		
Wed.		
Thurs.		
Fri.		

HABITS & STRATEGIES

If you need directions to a meeting place or appointment, save time and avoid an extra phone call by asking for directions when you set up the appointment. Write them on a Post-It note and stick in on your calendar. Once you make commitments, keep them so you won't waste time canceling and rescheduling.

HABITS & STRATEGIES

Try to group the appointments you do outside of your workplace so that you can do them all in one trip instead of running in and out of the office for separate appointments all week long. When someone asks for an appointment on a day you've decided "No appointments" say you're committed. Don't waste time on explanations. Maybe it will make sense for you to set aside a Wednesday afternoon for appointments and not return to the office after lunch, or maybe a Thursday morning before hitting the office would be your best bet.

Reevaluate, Revise, and Move On

"Lost time is never found again."
Benjamin Franklin

On Friday, review your weekly log and ask yourself, "Did this week's planning work for me? Did I like it?"

If you liked it, continue doing—and improving on—what worked. If you didn't like it, reevaluate and revise. Here are some dos and don'ts.

Do

1. Credit yourself for what you've accomplished.

2. Start a new and improved master-list plan for the coming week.

3. Valutize and write on your new plan everything that needs doing the following week along with all still-important unfinished items from the just-completed week.

Don't

1. Waste your time on guilt about what you didn't get done.

2. Feel frustrated and overwhelmed by your uncompleted master-list plan.

3. Expect at the end of any week to have *everything* done. Remind yourself again and again that the thing that's really important is to get the *right* things done.

Time management can be a challenge, so give yourself time to fine-tune your time. You can't always catch up on everything, and you won't get it right all at once. But enjoy what you do as you go.

There's no point in saving minutes and hours if you don't take genuine pleasure in your time and life.

Checkpoints

You have filled in a weekly planning questionnaire in order to come to grips with your framework for the coming week.

You have learned how to valutize your week's objectives, weeding out nonessentials and focusing on the *right* actions.

You have created a master-list plan to give yourself hands-on control of your time management.

You have discovered the importance of keeping *one* inclusive calendar containing all work and personal commitments as well as the value of a scribble pad.

You have constructed a weekly log based on your valutized master-list plan to help you focus on where your time is spent and to aid you in planning more effectively in the future.

In the next chapter, you will learn how to round out your daily and weekly planning with monthly and long-range planning.

The Big Picture: Stay in Control of Your Musts, Shoulds, and Want-To-Dos

INCLUDES

- Developing perspective and learning the difference between musts, shoulds, and wants

- Creating master lists for monthly or long-term planning

- Optimizing for the big picture

- Handling deadlines

- Taking advantage of top-energy time zones

- Working with others to make your time management system effective

- Measuring your big picture progress

FAST FORWARD

Develop Perspective ➤ *pp. 41–43*

- Realize that the always expanding number of choices you have when deciding what to spend your time on can lead to stress and frustration because you simply can't do it all.
- Enhance your knowledge about what you have time for, what you don't have time for, and what you want to have time for by recreating this information into a list of what must be done, what should be done, and what I want to get done.
- Refine your perspective on musts, shoulds, and want-to-dos by valutizing the list over and over again.
- Take a break, detaching yourself from your conclusions, and then rethink them as can-and-can't-dos, want-and-don't-want-to-dos and can-eliminates.

Monthly and Long-Range Planning ➤ *pp. 43–45*

- Chart your course with a master list of musts and shoulds including a breakdown of subtasks within each project as well as estimates of time needed and time available for each.
- Don't waste scheduling for want-to-dos, but tackle these bit by bit in the found minutes and hours of your days.

Optimize for Success ➤ *pp. 45–47*

- Use all the resources, skills, and good sense at your disposal to make the big-picture musts, shoulds, and want-to-dos on your agenda achievable.
- Develop habitual routines for repetitive tasks so they become like second nature and you can spend your time on the projects that require unrushed time and thought.
- Make valutizing again and again, and over and over, a number one habit.
- Ask continually, "What is the best use of my time right now?"

Deadlines ➤ pp. 47–50

- Test yourself to see how you currently approach deadlines—where you have keen focus and where you have shortfalls.
- Overcome *procrastination,* a major deterrent to meeting deadlines, by listing all the projects on which you have fallen prey to this harmful habit. Face the reasons that have stalled your forward momentum.
- Start your stalled engines on these projects by investing small increments of time that together will add up to increasingly productive hours.
- Recognize the perfectionist in yourself and understand that if you don't get a handle on your propensity to strive for absolute flawlessness in *every* job, you place all of your deadlines in jeopardy—just as you do if you procrastinate.

Take Advantage of High-Energy Time ➤ *pp. 50–51*

- Discover your peak periods of energy and tackle your most demanding jobs when you can benefit from your body's natural rhythm.
- Pace yourself, challenging your productivity at your best times, and clicking into routine and less taxing work when your energy wanes.
- Translate energy into enthusiasm and reap the rewards.

Working with Others ➤ *pp. 51–52*

- Recognize that often *your* objectives will be linked to a team project and that you will need to participate in a give-and-take relationship with others to meet your goals.
- Be flexible in designing your schedule and listen to suggestions from others to optimize everyone's success.

- Communicate—clearly and often—your needs and expectations and the agreed-upon timetable for completion of a joint endeavor.

Measure Your Progress ➤ *pp. 52–54*

- Devise a monthly progress report in which you recap your projections for each month and compare them to your accomplishments for the month.
- Appreciate the progress you have made.

You can't stop time by putting on the brakes of the 60-minutes-per-hour time train, so the only means for streamlining your way to your time management destination is to focus on the *big* view of what you need and want to do in the long haul down the track.

Time is the biggest asset you have in your days, weeks, and months, so as you gain speed with the earlier chapters' first-day and one-week time management tactics, keep your eye on the musts, shoulds, and want-to-dos that will help you get where you want to go on a long-range basis.

To break through the long-haul time crunch and reap the benefits, ask and answer the following questions:

What is most important to me in my use of time in the next month and year?

What *must* I do to accomplish this?

What *should* I do to accomplish this?

What do I *want* to do?

HABITS & STRATEGIES

You'll lose time rather than gain it if you do insufficient long-range planning. Planning will help you find time for your goals.

Develop a Good Perspective About Your Must, Should, and Want-To-Do Choices

When it comes to developing a good perspective on successful time management, accept the fact that in one lifetime there's not enough time to keep up with everything and get everything done. Instead of succumbing to stress and frustration about things for which there's no time, realize we're surrounded by too much exploding information and too many ever growing choices to have time for everything.

John P. Robinson of the University of Maryland and director of the Americans' Use of Time Project calls this "overchoice" and says the sheer number of options available to fill our time is overwhelming, whether we actually choose to do them or not.

How to Make Do-able Time Choices

The key to selecting the choices that are customized for you begins with reviewing your list of things I have time for, things I don't have time for, and things I want to have time for from Chap. 1. Using them as a starting point, create a new list of what must be done, what should be done, and what I want to get done.

I know! I know! This is more paperwork. But rather than turn on the tube or work on a word game, do yourself a favor and spend an hour on *this* game. It's a time investment that will give your objectives both precision and meaning.

"Until I made myself do this, many of my business goals and time frames were nothing more than aimless—'some days,' " a restaurant owner shared with me.

Once your objectives are on paper, you can

- Break them into subtasks
- Define the necessary steps to get started on them

MINUTES MATTER

Do it now!

Valutize Again—and Again and Again

Before you fill in the charts for projects, subtasks, time estimates, and dates on the upcoming master list for monthly and long-range planning, do the following five things. They'll help you refine your do-able view of what you *must, should,* and *want* to accomplish.

1. Determine the high-value and low-value worth for each must, should, and want-to-do.

2. Sit back and take a detached view of the results. Separate the findings into what you (a) can and can't do, (b) want and don't want to do, and (c) can eliminate.

3. Pinpoint what matters most so your time investment for each will be effective.

4. Try to find at least one objective you can cut out for which there would be no great loss if it didn't get done. Stare down this must, should, or want-to-do and forget about it.

5. Keep a list of the low-value tasks you don't want to eliminate and, whenever you have unexpected spare moments, choose one and work on small portions of it. When possible keep these low-value tasks as available as possible so you can pick them up at a moment's notice. An interior designer who wanted special cushions for the chairs in her office considered them a low-value task because her work with her clients came first. Her solution for finding time? She kept fabric, foam rubber pillow forms, scissors, pins, and needle and thread on the counter in her kitchen. Then she worked on the cushions in 10-minute spurts.

"You can be very busy without being effective. What's important is to learn how to do what matters most."
Hyrum W. Smith, chairman and CEO, Franklin Quest

Master Lists for Monthly and Long-Range Planning

Make copies of the following charts, allowing yourself as much space as you need. The scheduling tips in Chaps. 1 and 2 will be helpful in putting this master list into action. Refer to those tips as you need to.

Musts

Projects	Est. Time Needed	Available Time	Subtask Breakdown
1. _____	_____	_____	_____
2. _____	_____	_____	_____
3. _____	_____	_____	_____
4. _____	_____	_____	_____
5. _____	_____	_____	_____

Interim Dates	Due Dates
1. _____	_____
2. _____	_____
3. _____	_____
4. _____	_____
5. _____	_____

Shoulds

Projects	Est. Time Needed	Available Time	Subtask Breakdown
1. _____	_____	_____	_____
2. _____	_____	_____	_____
3. _____	_____	_____	_____
4. _____	_____	_____	_____
5. _____	_____	_____	_____

Interim Dates	Due Dates
1. _____	_____
2. _____	_____
3. _____	_____
4. _____	_____
5. _____	_____

Want-tos

There are no forms to fill in for your want-tos since they'll run the gamut from your loftiest ambitions to your lowest-value tasks. But whenever you have some dividend time, make minutes as well as hours count as you tackle small portions of the want-tos.

MINUTES MATTER

Question: *Where does time go?*
Answer: *Around the clock.*

20/20 Optimizers for Big-Picture Musts, Shoulds and Want-To-Dos

STEP BY STEP

1. Get busy and take your initial steps without waiting for the right time to start a job. When you wait for the right time, you end up so short of time you have to work long anxious hours to turn in a job that's far below your capabilities.

2. Locate a source of information you can trust to help you proceed if you don't know how to start.

3. Do one activity that leads to one long-term objective regularly.

4. Force yourself to find one hour at a time to devote to this objective—before work, after work, or at home in the early morning or late at night.

5. Establish habits for the fixed routine jobs you do over and over. You get them done faster by rote.

6. Identify what tasks you can handle as rush jobs and what jobs deserve your nonrush time.

7. Review your long-range planning master lists on a monthly and quarterly basis.

8. Spot-check your progress in between work sessions to see where you stand.

9. Revise your plans as necessary.

10. Develop both follow-up and feedback systems.

11. Be flexible.

12. Document your progress. This fortifies you to keep going.

13. Assign yourself the hardest tasks for the beginning of each week.

14. Try not to do too much all at once so projects don't look impossible.

15. Avoid jumping from one project to another as much as you can control this.

16. Give yourself a break when you have to spend the bulk of your time on the musts with no time for the shoulds. When this happens, don't feel guilty about the shoulds. Feeling guilty will only take more of your energy and time.

17. Keep on top of your valutizing. If you don't valutize constantly, you operate in a state of distraction—trying to do and be everything.

18. Remind yourself of projects you want to start or work on several weeks or months in the future by making a note, along with relevant information, on your calendar.

19. Know when you've done enough for one day. Your body and mind will give you signals. Your mind will slow up and your body will ache.

20. Ask yourself continually, "What is the best use of my time right now?"

HABITS & STRATEGIES

When it's time to get to work on whatever you have to do today start right in with the most important things immediately without postponing the big things in favor of easier small routine tasks that don't have to be done at that minute.

HABITS & STRATEGIES

Hang loose and remember that flexibility is the master key for opening the door to smart time management. No planning or timetable should be so rigid there's no way to do an about-face when the need arises.

How Well Do You Meet Deadlines?

Deadlines can be a positive push for moving along your musts, shoulds, and wants. But they *always* take longer than you think, so unless you get started in sufficient time, your time will be taken by other things. You'll be unable to meet them without sacrificing the quality of your work.

"If you are no longer stressing over the deadline, you will relax enough to move forward and actually tackle the task."
Steven Randall, management consultant

Rate yourself on how well you meet deadlines in the following test. Mark A for usually, B *for* sometimes, *and* C *for* never.

_____ Do you circle deadlines in red on your calendar?

_____ Do you find out what's expected of you from the person assigning a deadline so you don't waste time through poor communication?

_____ Do you ask for sufficient time to do a job?

_____ Do you suggest that people who give you deadlines prod you occasionally?

_____ Do you set your own deadlines if no one sets them for you?

_____ Do you stick with your self-set deadlines once you establish them?

_____ Do you map out the steps involved in a deadline, split the steps into a series of small deadlines, and calculate the amount of time each step will take?

_____ Are you realistic about how much you'll be able to accomplish in your work sessions for each step?

_____ Do you set your starting time for a date that will enable you to reach the finish line on time?

_____ Do you begin when you say you will—or even sooner—to build in some time for good measure?

_____ Do you monitor your time as you work and check your progress against your deadline?

_____ *Do you ask for more time to reschedule a deadline when your original one becomes the impossible dream?*

_____ *Do you create ways to postpone or minimize your other commitments in order to speed up a new deadline if you have to remake one?*

Scoring

Mostly *A* answers: *You're better than most busy people in meeting deadlines effectively.*

Primarily *B* answers: *You're partially focused on meeting deadlines, but there's room for improvement.*

Chiefly *C* answers: *You're receiving none of the benefits of keeping up with your deadlines.*

Two Gridlocks That Stall Deadlines: Procrastination and Perfectionism

Breaking through these gridlocks will help you avoid the time-losing crises that push you off the time track when a deadline is missed.

Procrastination

Procrastination is the thief of time. Collar him!

—*Charles Dickens*

"*Stop procrastinating and many crises will disappear.*"
Dr. Larry Baker, president, Time Management Center

Whatever the gender of procrastination, it's a major time issue problem because when you procrastinate, you

- Get behind before you start
- Feel unduly uneasy and stressed

Dr. Eugene Knott, a psychologist at the University of Rhode Island who teaches a course on overcoming procrastination, suggests coaching yourself through procrastination by becoming your own cheerleader and using positive self-talk to boost your interest or motivation. Here are other ways to get past this gridlock.

- Make a list of all the projects, tasks, and items on which you've been procrastinating.
- Figure out why you're procrastinating, e.g., hating a project, disliking the person who gave you the deadline, feeling overwhelmed by the pending

deadline, fearing you'll fail, waiting for the right time to start, or wanting to collect all details and necessary information before you start.

- Face whatever reason applies to you and, instead of letting the reason paralyze you, make yourself get started.
- Write on an index card the benefits you'll gain from beginning and finishing the job.
- Set aside half an hour a day to get started on what you've been putting off. This working for half an hour at a time will help get rid of your overwhelmed feeling and increase your momentum to work faster in each new half-hour stint. Besides, half-hour minutes add up to hourly totals.

Perfectionism

The price of perfection is prohibitive.

—*Sir Simon Marks, British retailing executive*

Having perfection as your goal is another reason for procrastination. But perfectionism is a giant time waster because, as we said in Chap. 1, for many deadlines, it's more important to turn in a *possible good* job on time than to hold back on the allotted timeframe while you strive for the *ideal perfect* job. Few jobs really justify the time and commitment it takes to make them perfect. Here are ways to cut back on perfectionism and gain time in the bargain.

- Recognize when a job needs to be done as perfectly as you can do it— and do it. But on the other hand, to paraphrase the serenity prayer, have the wisdom to know the difference between the needs-to-be-done-perfectly job and the general run of deadline jobs.
- Try to do the latter jobs right the first time around so you won't waste time doing them over. When you do have to change or redo some work, zero in to a quick-action fix-it just where the job needs reworking rather than going over the whole project again.
- *Let go* when it's time to let go. Be satisfied with an acceptable *good* job without holding back forever to take into account every detail you could include.
- Forgive yourself for imperfections and mistakes. "Ease up on yourself," advises Sunny Schlenger, a consultant on personal management and my coauthor on *How to Be Organized in Spite of Yourself.* "Where do you

get off thinking you're not human—not capable of overlooking something or making a mistake. Learn to forgive yourself."

HABITS & STRATEGIES

Cure an overdose of the perfectionism tendency by letting go and writing "Done" to a job that is good but not perfect. Then look at the "Done" job in two months to see whether taking the extra time to make it perfect would have made any real difference. Generally, you'll find that time puts perfectionism in the proper perspective.

Pace Yourself and Take Advantage of Your Top-Energy Time Zones

Rushing is addictive. Once hooked, it's hard to remember that the fastest way of doing things isn't always the best way. When hurried ask yourself, 'Do I really need to rush? What's the worst thing that can happen to me if I don't? Is that worse than what it's costing me to hurry?' Distinguish between necessary haste (late for an appointment) and mere impatience (one-hour photo developing).
Ralph Keyes, author of *Timelock: How Life Got So Hectic and What You Can Do About It*

When procrastination and perfectionism are deleted from your time squeeze, the next optimizer is matching your musts, shoulds, and want-to-dos to your energy levels. Science supports that everyone has varying degrees of energy during any given day, so pace yourself to gain the most value from your best time of day.

Do

1. Get to know your body's time clock and become familiar with your peak periods.

2. Respect your natural motivational energy levels at different times.

3. Determine where your energy wants to go at each level and arrange your schedule so you can do your most demanding and important tasks during the prime hours when you work most effectively.

4. Save your less demanding jobs for periods when you're low on energy.

5. Know when it's appropriate to pick up speed and when it's right to slow down.

6. Keep a grip on your speedup time and don't let it be a way of life that turns you into a victim of what's known as "hurry sickness." You can't work full time at a frenzied, fast-forward speed.

7. Set a minute-minder timer for the amount of time a job should take (plus some extra leeway minutes) and pace yourself to complete the job within the dictates of the timer.

Above all, turn your energy into enthusiasm.

MINUTES MATTER

Pay attention to where your energy wants to go minute by minute. You can get your work done faster and more precisely when you take advantage of your peak energy times.

You're *Not* a Loner— Time Management Won't Always Go Your Way

Though it's smart to control your time and your plans instead of constantly acquiescing to other people's demands, you can't ever have *complete* control of managing your time on the job. Since many projects depend on teamwork, you have to work with others, so there are things you can't control, along with the things you can. Here are approaches to keep in mind when you can't function on your own schedule at your chosen speed.

CAUTION

No man or woman is an island in managing time.

You Need Other People to Provide You with Input

- Expect to adapt and rearrange your plans and time frames to fit other people's schedules when necessary.

- Discuss with others any concerns and urgencies you have about projects you're working on with them.
- Check on what you need from your boss and coworkers before you need it.
- Listen to and act on other people's valid suggestions and regard them as supplements to your plans.

Other People Need You to Provide Them with Input

- Discuss—first thing in the morning—the jobs you want done with the people who will be doing them for you.
- Forget about making assumptions—others can't read your mind.
- Suggest people repeat their understanding of the directions you gave so no time will be lost on those tasks.
- Avoid holding up your coworkers' progress by employing your developing time management skills to meet the established deadline for *your* portion of a project.

HABITS & STRATEGIES

When you're under immense pressure to get a job completed—and too many people are demanding your time—shut your office door (if you have one), move to a vacant office or conference room, or work at home for a day.

Evaluate and Measure Your Big-Picture Progress

Periodically assess how well you're staying in control of your time management system by comparing your projections with your accomplishments on the following monthly progress report.

Keep thinking of the big picture as you appraise where you stand. Reflect on the positives of what you've done and celebrate how you're streamlining your way to your time management destination. Lighten up on yourself for the plans

STEP BY STEP

Monthly Progress Report

Projections

January	February	March

April	May	June

July	August	September

October	November	December

Accomplishments

January	February	March

April	May	June

July	August	September

October	November	December

"To regain control of your time, you may first need to adjust your attitude about time. Learn to live in the present by savoring the moment."
Lenora Yuen, psychologist

and projections you didn't get to in this time frame and know that because we're human—with our "reach exceeding our grasp"—we *never* get everything done. As a wise mentor once told me, "You'll be dead when that day comes!"

Checkpoints

You have achieved a perspective on the musts, shoulds, and want-to-dos on your plate.

You have mapped out a plan for tracking your long-term projects over a month or longer.

You have strengthened your long-range schedule by turning common activities into quick-to-complete routines and by consistently revalutizing larger objectives.

You have uncovered the reasons you procrastinate on certain projects and have taken steps to get back on track.

You have realized that being a perfectionist can be as detrimental as procrastination in meeting deadlines.

You have taken advantage of your top-energy time zone to optimize your productivity.

You have communicated clearly with others on jobs that require a team effort and planned effectively to meet the deadlines you are individually responsible for on the group project.

You have prepared a monthly report enabling you to record your accomplishments and progress as you proceed on multiple projects.

In the next chapter, you will see how to tip the time scales in your favor by organizing your workplace and paperwork to do more in less time.

Do More in Less Time: Workplace and Paperwork Optimizers

INCLUDES

- Taking an objective look at your workplace environment
- Giving your space a time-saving "face-lift"
- Choosing a paperwork system that matches your style
- Staying on top of what you need to read

FAST FORWARD

Take Charge of Your Space ➤ *p. 60*

- Look at the space in which you work through the eyes of a stranger and discover what changes immediately come to mind for improvement.

Eliminate Nonuseful Items ➤ *p. 61*

- Decide what objects are no longer contributing to your effectiveness in your work area.
- Remove niceties that don't really make a difference either personally or professionally and replace them with more helpful necessities.

Start with a Fresh Desktop ➤ *pp. 61–62*

- Clear your desktop of *everything*.
- Rearrange this primary workspace by replacing only those items that you need to use everyday, such as your phone and calendar. Remember that the most important thing on your desktop is the project at hand.

Clean Up Your Desk Drawers ➤ *pp. 62–63*

- Place only frequently used items in your desk drawers, grouping like items together in each drawer.
- Keep a litter drawer for collecting miscellaneous things that accumulate during the course of your work.
- Dump your litter drawer once a month, moving those items that have future value to an appropriate place and tossing the rest.

Find a Home for Your Equipment and Supplies ➤ *p. 63*

- Determine where equipment will be placed by the frequency of its use.
- Store needed supplies close to the equipment they belong with—for example, a supply of paper should be right next to your printer while floppy disks will be readily accessible next to your computer.
- Use utility shelves, pegboards, extra tables, Lucite boxes, or whatever else you find useful, as places to organize the excess materials that you want to be able to access quickly but not necessarily daily or even weekly.

Make Your Environment Comfortable ➤ *pp. 63–65*

- Decide what personal items are important to you in making the space in which you spend much of your day comfortable and productive.
- Choose items that enhance your well-being but do not distract from your work.

Come to Grips with Paperwork ➤ *p. 65*

- Personalize a system that works for you, but remember to *keep it simple.*
- Add an extra hour to your day, dedicated to cleaning up a neglected backlog of paperwork until you are on track again.

Categorize Your Mail ➤ *pp. 65–67*

- Organize mail files for incoming mail that you can use to sort your correspondence into groups requiring different actions on your part, such as "immediate response" or "file."
- Avoid a growing pile of correspondence that needs response (and, therefore, time) by customizing form letters when appropriate or jotting a quick answer to the sender right on the original letter or memo.
- Be concise in your memos, letters, and reports—less is better for your time *and* for your recipients.
- Employ the aid of an assistant, if possible, and allow him/her to take as much responsibility as you can in creating outgoing correspondence.

Organize Your Files ➤ *pp. 67–69*

- Throw away anything that you really don't need to keep.
- File often—daily if you can—and clearly label folders for quick retrieval.
- Purge your files regularly, archiving inactive information that may be needed at a much later date.
- Consider the use of a day-by-day tickler file matched to your musts, shoulds, and want-to-dos as a way of keeping needed information close at hand as well as serving as a daily reminder of important actions that need to be taken.
- Remove work-in-progress files from your desk and store them in portable containers, such as stackable crates, limiting one project to one container.
- Color-code project files so that you can quickly pull out just what you need to work on from your work-in-progress file.

Use Your Rolodex Wisely ➤ *p. 69*

- Staple business cards directly onto Rolodex cards, avoiding the time needed to write out the same information over again.
- Use the back of cards to remind yourself of useful information connected with the person on the front.

Track Your Finances ➤ *p. 70*

- Take a quiz to determine how well you are doing at maintaining good financial records linked to your work and life.

Learn to Speed Read ➤ *pp. 71–72*

- Limit your professional reading to publications that give you the most value for your time.
- Highlight items of interest while you read—don't put yourself in the position of having to reread to mark important information.
- Tote material that you need to read around with you—there are always found moments while waiting for meetings, waiting for trains, or while you commute on public transportation.
- Listen to reading material on tape, when it's available.

When you set up your workplace for *your* convenience—and your workflow and traffic patterns—it's easier to manage your time. It's also easier to stay on track when, as part of your workplace, you have a simple what-to-keep, where-to-keep-it, and how-to-find-it paperwork system.

To cut down on your time stress, take full advantage of this chapter's time-tested ways to arrange your office and plow through the paperwork blizzard that literally blows your mind. Then move on to Chap. 5 to get on another time track that will introduce you to high-tech devices for doing more in less time.

View Your Workspace from the Objective Eyes of a Stranger Seeing It for the First Time

It's easy to get accustomed to things as they always were. And in this blindfolded mental state, we try to function in spaces that don't do all they could do to facilitate our use of time.

The way to move on from this human trait is to take an extended minute to look at your space from the fresh perspective of a person who has never seen it before. You'll notice all kinds of improvements to make, whether you work in a cubbyhole or a corner office.

The following step-by-step workplace time-savers will help you improve your workplace arrangements, though naturally not all busy people will face-lift their space in identical ways. Customize what's right for you, and your space, situation, and workstyle.

Workplace Time-Savers— Step by Step

Eliminate Outdated and Useless Space-Fillers

Step 1: Eliminate all distracting accoutrements you may be overlooking that have outlived their time and contribute nothing to your work or enjoyment. With a new detachment, determine what objects you don't need or use that you could get rid of to gain more working space. A graphic artist discovered she'd overlooked a valuable and much-needed spot on which to spread out her work when she got rid of a dried flower arrangement that had been gathering dust on a table for at least five years. A purchasing agent found needed space for an extra bulletin board when he took down a composite of pictures from his now-adult son's Little League days.

Look around your office in your next free minute and fill in the following:

"The art of being wise is the art of knowing what to overlook."
William James, philosopher

What Five Things Have I Overlooked that I Can Eliminate?

First, _____

Second, _____

Third, _____

Fourth, _____

Fifth, _____

After you justify five potentials, be merciless. Do away with them!

Refurbish Your Desktop

Step 2: Move everything off your before *desktop for a fresh start.* Remove paper piles, in and out boxes, work-in-progress piles, stationery supplies, lamps, miscellaneous notes, telephone messages, current and accumulated mail, your planner/organizer/calendar/scribble pad, and anything else that makes it impossible to *see* the top of your desk. Place the contents in labeled cardboard boxes (or other containers we discuss later).

Step 3: Put your after *desktop back in order by retaining only the things you use every day and rearranging them for a better tomorrow.* A neat desktop contributes to thinking more clearly, so give yourself this time-gaining plus by going through the boxes and putting back on your desktop only the following items:

Your phone (on the side of the desk that's most accessible for you)

Your Rolodex

Your planner/organizer/calendar/scribble pad

A basket or plastic container for pens, pencils, highlighters, eraser, scissors, stapler, postage stamps, Post-Its, tape, glue, rubber stamp, memo pad, and paperclips

A minimal number of non-space-taking personal items that are important to you. An egg timer that acts as a reminder to keep my phone calls short is an essential for me. A one-hour minute minder helps me pace myself as I work.

In addition, consider replacing your in and out boxes with a triple stackable tray (or if you prefer a small vertical file) on one side of your desk. Use one section for immediate musts, the second for less urgent tasks that shouldn't be out of sight, and a third for items that are ready to leave your desktop. Most important of all—*remember that the rest of your desktop is for just one thing: the primary job you're working on!* You'll be more productive when you don't face a combination of projects that clutter up your desktop and demand fragmented attention.

Heighten the Usefulness of Your Desk Drawers

Step 4: Go through your desk drawers with this five-point action plan:

1. Look at your desk drawers objectively, just as you looked at your desktop.

2. Determine which drawers should contain what for quick accessibility.

3. Clear out one drawer at a time. Remove the contents, sort through them, and reserve and put back the things you use frequently but not daily. Do this until each drawer is done.

4. Move materials you use only periodically out of your desk area to a spot where you can find them fast when you need them. Clear

Lucite boxes, appropriately labeled, provide excellent storage for this material.

5. Allow yourself *one* disorder litter drawer as a refuse heap for the miscellany that seems to have no special home when it appears on your desk. Once a month empty the litter drawer completely. Find a home for items that need one and toss what's left in the refuse can. Then begin anew with a clean litter drawer.

Place the Equipment That Supports Your Work in Convenient Locations

Step 5: Place your equipment and supplies in advantageous and available spots. How frequently specific equipment and supplies are used will define where to place them so you have access to them in minutes. Have your computer and printer and everything related to them in one spot. If you use a tape recorder (and telephone pick-up device), have that near your phone. Similarly, if your work requires other dictating equipment, place that strategically. Do the same for your answering machine/voice mail, copier (if you have one), and transcriber (if you use one).

Over and above the standard bookcase you undoubtedly have, quick-to-assemble utility shelves provide extra storage space for magazines and other publications plus items that aren't a good fit for your bookcase or files. Pegboards give you access to visual reminders that don't belong elsewhere, while tables covered with a floor-length felt cloth hide what you don't want visible and use only once in a while.

Two Other Reminders

Do: Keep your equipment in good shape

Don't: Continue to use outdated equipment

Personalize Your Space

Step 6: Make your surroundings enjoyable and comfortable. Pleasant surroundings optimize both your time and productivity because you're more into working when you like the place where you work. To make your place user-friendly and enhance your sense of well-being, supplement the standard and practical office items with your personal touches.

Naturally, if you work for an employer, rather than yourself, many furnishings will be preselected. But there are things you can have (or ask for) that will add to your comfort and pleasure. Following is a baker's dozen of choices for an eclectic mix. Select the ones that are right for you.

CAUTION

Don't allow any unused furnishings or equipment to take up space in your workplace.

As you make your selections, however, be sure to avoid such space-taking items as the graphic artist's tired dried flowers and the purchasing agent's outdated pictures. Instead go for

1. A good quality ergomatically designed office chair. Models that swivel or move on castors make it easy and quick to move from one spot to another.
2. A lamp that provides good lighting and ambiance.
3. Photographs.
4. Art.
5. Meaningful memorabilia (but not the refrigerator variety).
6. An armoire or credenza.
7. A hanging magazine and newspaper rack.
8. Bookcases.
9. A colorful quilt or Indian or Mexican blanket on the wall.

HABITS & STRATEGIES

If your bookcase is in disarray, take all the books off the shelves and put them in piles on the floor. When the bookcase is empty go through the unorganized piles and arrange the books into categorized piles, according to subject matter. When you put them back leave shelf space for adding new books in the right category. This avoids the hit-or-miss habit of putting your latest acquisitions wherever they happen to land.

10. Epigrams that inspire you.

11. Small antique accessories.

12. A collection of coffee mugs from faraway places.

13. Good silk plants (silk won't take watering time).

The What-to-Keep, Where-to-Keep-It, and How-to-Find-It Paperwork System

Just as people don't organize their workplaces in identical styles, neither do they wade through paperwork blizzards in a one-rule-for-everyone manner. But there's one rule that works for *everyone* that *everyone* needs to follow: *choose simplicity!*

With that in mind, if you've reached the point of a paperwork disaster, arrive at work an hour early or stay an hour late for a week, or as long as it takes. An alternative can be a weekend or two. In that committed time, the following step-by-step plan can get you on track with your paperwork, no matter how derailed you are.

A Paperwork Plan—Step by Step

Incoming and Outgoing Mail
Incoming

STEP BY STEP

- Have your mail screened by an assistant before it comes to you, if there's someone to do this for you.
- When it comes to you, set up mail files by sorting and separating the mail into the five categories suggested in Chap. 1: for immediate response, to go over later, to read more thoroughly, to file, to throw out.
- Try to make a decision on your first reading about what to do with each piece. Then place each piece in labeled stackable trays that stay off your desk. Use colored labels for each tray: red for for immediate response; blue for to go over later; green for to read more thoroughly; and orange for to file. Don't bother with a throw out file—that category deserves the trash can treatment.

MINUTES MATTER

Open your mail near the wastebasket and dump junk mail in it at once.

- Insure your immediate response file against bulging by jotting a fast answer to the sender on the original letter or replying on a speed memo or business postcard you've had printed for quick responses.
- Write ideas for your responses to other mail in the margins of the correspondence that goes into your mail files. This will save rereading time later.
- Compose form letters you can personalize to fit a variety of situations.

MINUTES MATTER

A quick phone call is often faster than writing a memo.

Outgoing

- Send people less-is-more memos, letters, and reports. In addition to saving you time, brief messages and reports are more likely to be read.
- Authorize an assistant to compose answers and reply to as much mail as possible. If the assistant sends you mail he or she could handle, send it back with a note "Please take care of this."
- Use a tape recorder or dictating device for letters and reports you have to handle yourself before passing them on to a helper.
- Organize your thoughts before you dictate so you won't waste time while dictating.
- Consolidate your correspondence and dispose of all you can in one sitting.

Once accumulated mail is under control, do the preceding steps on a daily basis.

MINUTES MATTER

Avoid loitering over your mail. Don't let it become a time-taking ritual.

HABITS & STRATEGIES

Slow down the influx of junk mail and unwanted catalogs by sending companies postcards stating you want your name taken off their lists. This requires extra minutes, but it's worth pursuing and persisting.

Setting Up a Filing System
File-Cabinet Filing

- Before you put *anything* in your main file cabinets, decide what to retain and what to throw away. To make sure your active files don't become a paper wasteland, answer these "should I file it?" questions:

  Do I really need this piece of paper?

  How much would it matter if I didn't hang on to it?

  How difficult would it be to find the information elsewhere?

- Determine where material should be filed as it comes to you. Attach a Post-it note with this information as a reminder to you or a helper.
- File daily as much as possible.

CAUTION

Label Everything

- Label every folder clearly so you can retrieve information quickly.
- Cross-reference
- Have some empty file folders in the front of your file drawers and set up a new file as soon as you have paperwork related to a new subject.
- Clear out the old to make room for the new regularly. Purge all you can by asking yourself whether you've used the material in the past year. If the answer is no, remove the material from your active files and store dated papers you may need to keep in archive files (preferably away from your workplace).
- Maintain an inventory of your file drawers in the front of each file. Photocopy the lists and put them in a folder labeled *file inventory.*
- Date all paperwork and action taken.

Tickler Files and Everyday File Sorters

"Each time you consult a file folder, riffle through it quickly to pick out and throw away the dead wood."

Stephanie Winston, founder of The Organizing Principle

Enroute to their ultimate resting places, some papers can be kept—temporarily—in tickler files or everyday file sorters. If a tickler file is attractive to you as an extra means of staying on track, get 31 file folders and label one for each day of the month. Put notations of everything relevant to that day in the appropriate folder, along with such things as greeting cards to send and other musts, shoulds, and want-to-dos you may or may not have designated elsewhere.

Another alternative, an everyday file sorter, can be purchased at office supply stores. If you choose this as part of your temporary paperwork system, use it for the following items:

- Information relating to incoming or outgoing phone calls
- Letters and memos you need to write
- Questions that require answers
- Topics to bring up at meetings and conferences
- Items to take to appointments

At the end of each day, move what you need and haven't used to the next day's tickler file or sorter, or file it permanently if you want to retain it. Throw it away if you don't.

Work-in-Progress Files

A major problem of *before* desktops is the work-in-progress piles, predestined to overwhelm you as long as they stay on your desk. The best and *only* solution, as suggested previously, is to move these piles off your desk and place them in special containers. Here are five suggested containers. Select the type that appeals to you and put everything for one project in the container labeled for that. Choose from the following:

1. Large baskets.

2. Plastic crates from office supply stores. (I pile one crate on top of another and use four for four works in progress.)

3. Clear Lucite boxes.

4. Vinyl briefcases.

5. Rolling carts with stacked plastic baskets.

For visual aids you may want to distinguish the various stages of your work in progress with a different-colored paper or file folder for each progression of your work. A benefit of these containers is that each is portable. You can move them whenever and wherever you choose.

Leave space in your briefcase or carry-all for portions of work-in-progress projects (and other paperwork) that you can do away from the office. Make sure to have pens, pencils, highlighters, and a pad for ideas and notes. I also see that my briefcase contains scissors, paperclips, a small stapler, tape, envelopes, and stamps. Clear out your briefcase periodically. That's every bit as important as clearing your desk and files.

HABITS & STRATEGIES

Set up special files (or secure containers) for all information pertaining to taxes, investments, equipment purchases, insurance, your pension and other financial matters.

Rolodex Maximizers

If you think of your Rolodex as strictly for addresses, do a double take and think again. You can save many minutes of accessing information by making your Rolodex a high-value, hands-on time-saver. Time management gurus recommend including, at the end of *Z*, extra cards that contain information you need to find quickly, e.g., social security numbers as well as driver's license, credit card, bank card, and insurance policy numbers.

To save time on filing business cards (and to know where to find them when you need them), tape them to blank Rolodex cards. Use the back of all of the cards for pertinent information about the person whose name is on the front. Include reminders or any helpful information such as birthdays, anniversaries, a client's favorite restaurant, name of assistant (or person's spouse and/or children), and directions to meeting places, offices, or homes.

Even if you use electronics for contacts' names and addresses, you'll want a Rolodex, too. Keep it up to date by weeding out cards that are no longer relevant.

Stay on Top of Financially Related Paperwork

Take this test to see how well you're staying on top. Put checks (√) in the appropriate spots.

	Never	Sometimes	Always
1. Do you keep track of business expenses as they accrue to speed up preparing your monthly expense report?	_____	_____	_____
2. Do you maintain monthly tax records to be halfway there at tax time?	_____	_____	_____
3. Do you put bills-to-pay on a spindle, in a special envelope, or on your computer so you won't lose time hunting for them?	_____	_____	_____
4. Do you use automatic bill-paying arrangements?	_____	_____	_____
5. Do you submit medical bills for reimbursement regularly?	_____	_____	_____
6. Do you use health insurance plans and providers that minimize paperwork?	_____	_____	_____
7. Do you keep photocopies of credit cards and the contents of your wallet in a secure place?	_____	_____	_____
8. Do you keep abreast of your investments, insurance coverage, and overall financial planning?	_____	_____	_____
Totals	_____	_____	_____

Scoring: *If most of your answers are* Always, *give yourself a plus mark for your financial time management. If you have 50 percent or more* Sometimes *answers, consider yourself between a plus and a minus. If you have 50 percent or less, you definitely have a minus mark and need to develop better time skills for financial paperwork.*

A Reading Plan—Step by Step

STEP BY STEP

Reading for information is a big part of paperwork, so here's a master list for managing your reading time.

1. Restrict the amount of reading material you hope to cover. With today's ever growing information explosion, you can't read, know, and absorb everything.

2. For career purposes, read only the magazines, newspapers, books, and business and trade publications that give you the greatest value for your reading time.

3. Skim the table of contents of publications to spot the material that interests you. Tear out that material and save time and space by getting rid of the rest of the publication. If the publication isn't yours, photocopy the pieces you want to read.

4. Carry items you plan to read with you so you can peruse it during waiting-time minutes, going to and from work, or standing in long lines.

5. Fill a reading basket with secondary material you want to go through. Keep the basket close to you as a visible reminder.

6. Distribute reading material among your coworkers (and have them do the same) so you can share and exchange what you learn with each other.

7. When you're ready to read but have limited time, reading experts suggest reading only headlines or titles, first paragraphs, topic sentences of each paragraph, and endings. This will give you the key information.

8. Use your highlighter to mark important items the first time you read something.

9. Stop magazine subscriptions when you can't keep up with current issues.

10. Throw (or give) away any *to read* stack that's six months old if you haven't touched it.

"Resolve to edge in a little reading every day, if it is but a single sentence. If you gain fifteen minutes a day, it will make itself felt at the end of the year."
Horace Mann, educator

11. Listen to some reading material on tape while doing other things.

12. Take a speed-reading course.

13. Read every day.

Make "Clean Out and Let Go" Your Mantra

Once you've arranged your workplace and plowed through your paperwork, persevere with the progress you've made. It only takes a few minutes at the close of your working day to straighten up the top of your desk and put away any papers that didn't get placed in their designated spots as soon as you finished with them. Then every six months, take a new look at your workplace and paperwork. This will benefit you for all of your life in your race against time.

Checkpoints

You have rearranged your working environment, creating a space that is comfortable, functional, and efficient.

You have tackled the explosion of paperwork that has slipped from your control.

You have designed a system for expeditiously handling both incoming and outgoing mail.

You have learned to gain more in less time from your reading material.

In the next chapter, you will see how to work faster and smarter by using the *when* and *how* high-tech devices that are right for you.

Know Computer and Hi-tech When and How Time-Savers

INCLUDES

- Learning the difference between time-gaining and time-wasting technology
- Using a contact manager program
- Choosing a portable electronic organizer such as a PIM or PDA
- Profiting from the benefits of a fax/modem
- Discovering the time-gaining advantages of the Internet
- Recognizing other technological solutions that provide alternative help in the battle against time
- Finding the balance between paper and technology
- Identifying the *when* and *how* of technology time-savers

FAST FORWARD

Know Your Options ➤ *pp. 77–78*

- Become familiar with the range of technological tools available to you.
- Ask yourself what benefits you expect and need from each piece of hardware or software that you consider incorporating into your time-gaining strategy.

Contact Managers ➤ *pp. 79–80*

- Consider the value of a computerized program that will organize your calendar, to-do list, and name and address book all in one place.
- Decide whether or not your computer is the best tool for reminding you to make important phone calls or keep appointments.
- Understand that the value of a contact manager is only as good as the careful input and maintenance of information that you provide and type in.

Portable Electronic Organizers ➤ *pp. 80–81*

- Compare the features of electronic organizers, personal information managers (PIMs), and personal digital assistants (PDAs) and determine which is most suited to your needs.
- Realize that effective use of any portable organizer is minimized if it is not used in tandem with your desktop computer.
- Transfer all data from notes, memos, and to-do lists to your desktop files on a regular basis.

Faxes and Modems ➤ *pp. 82–83*

- Ensure that your computer is equipped with either an internal or external modem to facilitate quick and easy communication with others.

- Use your computer's fax/modem in place of a stand-alone fax machine to speed up sending and receiving time-sensitive material.

The Internet ➤ pp. 83–85

- Take advantage of the easy-to-use features of e-mail for as much correspondence as possible, thus avoiding the many extra steps and time needed for snail mail.
- Explore the features of commercial, library, or university online services to determine which aspects will provide you the most benefit for the least amount of time invested.
- Surf the Web for unlimited access to resources and information from around the world.
- Find newsgroups within the UseNet that dovetail with your needs and use them to make many contacts that can benefit your business.

More Technological Solutions ➤ pp. 85–87

- Consider using a scanner if your projects require working with numerous documents from printed sources that will be accessed more readily when organized in a computerized file.
- Record your thoughts or ideas as they occur to you with a small portable tape recorder. This is a great way to get a jump start on time-consuming memos and letters.
- Use a headset when you are on lengthy phone calls to free your hands and allow you to do small tasks while you talk.
- Organize your financial records by installing and using an automated financial management program in your computer.
- Avoid the horror of lost work by regularly backing-up your files on your hard drive.
- Keep an extra set of floppies with your backed-up work at an alternative site to your office—just in case.

Balancing Paper and Technology ➤ *pp. 87–89*

- Decide what works best for you from the potpourri of choices available and then make sure that both computerized and nonelectronic systems complement each other.
- Incorporate dates into your file names as a quick and easy reference for finding the right file.

Identify the When and How ➤ *pp. 89–92*

- Employ the help of a knowledgeable person to assist you in deciding on what programs and products best suit your specific needs.
- Evaluate your present time-saving systems and the changes you want to make before making any hardware or software purchases.
- Write down your needs for and expectations of the new product you are considering and take this list with you to the computer store.
- Give yourself time to learn and implement the necessary skills when you upgrade to a new technological solution—loss of time learning up front translates to more time gained forever after.

There's no way to escape technology as a constantly developing tool for enhancing time management skills. Each year it picks up more and more speed and moves ahead on such a fast track that lagging behind in a waiting room on the trip to Hi-Tech Land will derail you from using the time-saving electronics that help you streamline your time.

Still, there's a caution sign that you *have* to keep in mind because technology can consume enormous amounts of time without producing comparable returns—*unless you're extremely selective about when and how it can benefit you and save and gain you time.*

To get a broad range of views on this, I talked to a variety of consultants and teachers who train people to use technology in ways that will save them time. I asked about the whens and hows and also about the products they themselves and other busy people use.

Generally speaking, I've refrained from naming specific products because of the many choices in the marketplace. But to help you find a light at the end of the tunnel, I've included a mini list of the choices experts and users talked about most, at the conclusion of this chapter.

What's the Bottom Line between Time-Gaining and Time-Wasting Technology?

Technology is the ultimate time-saving tool and, along with computers, most workplaces have speed-dialing phones, speaker phones, teleconferencing, answering machines, voice mail, copiers, fax machines, modems, and e-mail to make you more productive. You yourself may have, on your own, a car phone, cellular phone, or pager. To complement this technology, there are additional hardware products, such as electronic organizers, and software titles, such as contact managers or financial programs, to aid you in your efforts. Online services and the Internet further enhance your time-saving options.

To select the technology that's right for you from today's electronic smorgasbord (and to make life easier instead of more complex), the fine line between using time-gaining and time-wasting technology depends on identifying *specifically* the following:

1. Why you want and need a product or program

2. What you expect it to do for you

"The primary consideration is 'Will it work for you?' " advised Stephanie Denton, a professional organizer, owner of Denton & Company, and a teacher of time management techniques.

"Technology is a great tool as long as you're comfortable with it and use it in a way that is right for you. Some people like to write a lot and want their planners on paper rather than a computer. Others want everything on their computer. You need to find the combination that fits your style and worklife."

As an example of this, Denton tells the story of three clients at the same company who had the same job titles and the same job functions.

One was very technology-oriented, kept her software planner on her computer and used e-mail exclusively for communicating with other people. The second client was a 50/50 user between computer and paper systems but admitted to feeling more comfortable having her planner and to-do list in paper form. The third did practically everything on paper and preferred communicating verbally with her boss and other people rather than sending messages back and forth by e-mail.

Before we discuss what you can do to identify your personal needs, let's look at the electronics that maximize your time when they're the right hi-tech for you and you use them effectively.

MINUTES MATTER

Say "no" to technology that overcomplicates your life and takes more time than it saves.

Contact Management Programs

A *contact manager* is software with database capabilities that loads your daily planner into your computer and has many functions, such as organizing and coordinating your calendar, daily schedule, appointments, to-do list, and name and address book. You can print out this material whenever you want hard copies.

Once you type in information about the persons with whom you do business (along with notes regarding your communications with them), a contact manager automatically keeps track of your *people* leads. In some programs, you only have to type the first few letters of individuals' names to find out immediately all you need to know about them.

There are many good programs on the market, though some have more capabilities than others. For example, some are programmed with a message alert, phone call alert, and scheduling and meeting alert. Once you turn them on in the morning, they'll beep five minutes before you have to do something.

"The advantage of a contact management system over a paper system is that all information can be in one place," explained Debbie Gilster, a small business consultant and owner of Organize & Computerize. "The computer will help you remember what you need to do when you need to do it. When you have a contact to make three months in the future a reminder to call that person will pop up on the screen at that time."

A contact manager can also save you the time of getting material out of file drawers and then refiling it.

"Rather than having to look in file drawers for papers, you can quickly retrieve information on the computer and save a couple of hours a week," says Jann Jasper, a time and paper management consultant who teaches how to spend time effectively through the use of computers. "You can give the computer a key word and when you're finished with the information, all you have to do is close the screen."

Four Ways to Make Contact Managers Gain Time for You

1. Investigate available programs before you buy to be sure their functions and capabilities match the tasks you want the program to do.

2. See that the program is set up properly and get help if you have problems doing this yourself.

3. Be meticulous about typing vital information into the program.

4. Discipline yourself to stick with it during the learning process.

HABITS & STRATEGIES

Expect to invest time in mastering new technology. In the beginning, it will take time. But as long as you are learning the right technology for you, you end up saving time.

Electronic Organizers, Personal Information Managers, and Personal Digital Assistants

These handheld computers which you can carry with you are called by different names: electronic organizers, personal information managers (PIMs), and personal digital assistants (PDAs). They're small enough to slip into a briefcase or purse and lighter to tote than a laptop. They have similar functions to contact managers, though they're usually more limited in scope. Some have more functions than others. Whatever their functions are, it's important to transfer the information you put into them to your desktop computer when you return to your desk.

Electronic Organizers

These devices are designed to store memos, addresses, phone numbers, and schedules. They also have a calendar and to-do list.

"I'm trying to eliminate paper as much as I can, so my electronic organizer is my portable brain," says Donna McMillan, founder of McMillan & Company Professional Organizing. "I've been on it for three years, and it's my life. By using the memo section of my organizer I have portable notes. God forbid I ever lost the data on my organizer, so I back it up to the hard drive of my computer regularly."

Personal Information Managers (PIMs)

A PIM goes a step further than a simple electronic organizer and, along with including memo functions, an address book, calendar, phone numbers, to-do list, and schedules, it has reminder alarms for appointments and events. You can sort your to-do lists and print your schedules.

"My PIM keeps me as close to being organized as I'm likely to get," reported Franklynn Peterson, coauthor of the syndicated newspaper column *The Business Computer.* "The relational database part of the program stores names, numbers, notes, whatever. The calendar is displayed in diverse formats—weekly, monthly, or daily—depending on how much stuff is crammed into it.

"I also configure the color of various items to my psychological quirks—for instance, red for to-do items. When I'm finished with the to-do items I click 'Done' and they turn dull gray. I schedule appointments individually or in groups. Every Monday, Wednesday, and Friday at 4:30, a message beeps and pops up over whatever is on the screen to tell me to go to the health club."

HABITS & STRATEGIES

Join a computer users' group to share and obtain knowledge of technology that's important to you. This will save you hours of trying to unravel problems yourself.

Personal Digital Assistants (PDAs)

PDAs are one of the fastest-growing segments in technology and, even though some models have usability flaws that manufacturers are working on, these devices are amazing in all that they can do. Along with the usual address book, calendar, phone numbers, other lists, and memo functions, their manufacturers promise they can serve as a phone, fax machine, modem, and pager. People report using them to track meetings, respond to messages, and fine-tune documents.

"I can take notes, easily transfer them back to my PC, and work on them there," said Greg Ruff, a high-tech consultant and vice president of General Automation, who carries his PDA *everywhere.* "It's much more efficient for me to do that than to carry scraps of paper around."

Fax Machines and Modems

Modems

A *modem* is the device that connects your computer to a telephone line. It can be a separate unit, connected to your computer with a cable (external), or built directly inside your computer (internal). Both types of modems enable you to do the following:

1. Communicate with other people

2. Get into online information services, search thousands of databases, and receive limitless information

3. Send and receive e-mail and computer files

4. Send and receive faxes

The more bits per second (bps) your modem is capable of, the faster it will send and deliver information. Because maximizing your time-saving is important, the speed of a modem should be an important criteria when making a purchase of this advantageous hardware.

Fax Machines

You don't have to be a hi-tech wiz to be user-friendly with a fax machine since the choice of whether to use one is usually made for you in today's business environment. Undoubtedly, you're well aware of the two ways to fax—with a stand-alone fax machine or a fax modem with your PC. The latter is an excellent choice when minutes matter for the following reasons:

1. You don't have to waste time creating and printing hard copies to transmit.

2. You don't have to leave your computer to step across the office to the fax machine, since the computer will send the document you've created right from your computer.

3. You can receive incoming faxes directly at your desk and computer rather than having them pile up and sit in a box by the communal fax machine.

Moreover, the computer's fax administrator is always at the ready to send and receive messages on your screen at any time of day. You never have to wait for people who beat you to the fax machine to fax their material first.

The Internet—Ready or Not!

The Internet is a worldwide transmission line for presenting information and sending and receiving it in electronic form. Once you're trained and experienced in using this network of computer and telephone lines, you can find electronic phone books, stock prices, newspaper and magazine articles, research studies, government documents, technical reports, Supreme Court decisions, statistics, business reports, weather reports, and much more varied information.

Here are some of the Net's time-savers and gainers.

E-mail

"E-mail is the greatest timesaver that has been invented since the answering machine."
Alison Berke, president of bworks.com, an Internet development company that designs websites

E-mail is a great time-saver because, rather than maintaining a "correspondence to answer" folder, then writing a letter, addressing an envelope, buying and attaching a stamp, and mailing the letter, you can simply type an addressee's name and your message on your computer, press a Send button and have your message on its way in a minute.

"Besides being a physical time-saver, it's a mental stress reducer, too, because you know people are going to get your messages whether or not they're there at the time," stated Alison Berke, president of bworks.com, an Internet development company that designs websites and helps users navigate their way through the Internet. "It can eliminate time zones, busy signals, answering machines, and voice mail. It also avoids 'If you would like to talk to so-and-so press 1, et cetera.'"

Online Services

Online services are your ticket to focused, preorganized information searches. Some of the services are the commercial ones for which you pay a monthly fee. Others are public and university libraries that have their catalogs online. The databases within the services provide entry to all major professional, business, and popular publications.

Valuable interactive functions of online services include discussions, forums, and bulletin boards on a wide range of subjects. They also provide chat rooms in which you can talk live with people around the world by inputting messages and receiving replies. These features offer you the opportunity to gather information or insights from others logged on to the same discussion. Often they provide helpful hints or ideas about a particular item of interest to you.

You can also gain time with library or university online services because, even though it can take a while to get online and find information, this saves the time of going to the library in person. On the other side of the coin, when you're on unfamiliar ground with online services, a reference librarian and experienced online researcher can sometimes get you the information you want in minutes and save you the time of doing it yourself.

The World Wide Web

The Web (http://www.) is a method of organizing thousands and thousands of sites in which documents residing on the Internet are connected to each other through words in the document that act as gateways to other related documents.

You use a Web browser program to "surf the Net," and since Web sites cover every imaginable subject you can search for almost any topic that interests you. Web sites can be set up by anyone, and some of the online services permit you to create your own personal or business site.

"If you have your own business you can save time serving customers if you're on the Web," advises Alison Berke. "When you hand out your business card with your http://www. on it people can always find you quickly and get information about what you do."

HABITS & STRATEGIES

Set time limits on your online searches so you don't waste minutes and hours obtaining information for which you have no use. Like eating peanuts one after another, nonstop online searching leads to plugging into things you don't need or want. Differentiate between what you can get and what you will use.

Search Engines and Directories

You can explore the Net through the search engines that are well-indexed directories of Web pages. Since they organize information in categories, you can search for classifications by keywords. Among the most popular search engines and directories are Alta Vista, Infoseek, Webcrawler, and Yahoo.

The Usenet

This giant global text bulletin board (often called the world's largest bulletin board) contains articles composed and transmitted by Net users. There are thousands of *newsgroups* (topic headings for the interest groups in Usenet). When you choose the newsgroup that interests you, you find news you don't discover anywhere else. Each day more than 50,000 articles appear on the Usenet.

So where does time management come into this?

Along with supplying information you can often use, the Usenet is a means of having your messages read by thousands and thousands of people. If mailings are a part of your work, you can save the time and labor of compiling a list of potentially interested people by posting to the appropriate newsgroup.

More Technological Solutions for Time Drains

As mentioned at the start of this chapter, everyone is familiar with the time-saving technology of speed-dialing phones, car phones, cellular phones, speaker phones, teleconferencing, answering machines, voice mail, copiers, and pagers. But there are still other programs and products that can streamline your time. Here are more to think about—though not everyone needs *everything* that's technologically available.

Scanners

A *scanner,* which is a piece of hardware, allows you to scan typewritten and published text, as well as pictures, from paper into your computer through the use of *optical character recognition (OCR)* software. When you want a paperless office or are confronted with projects demanding time-consuming retyping of photocopies, faxed material, magazine articles, and other research material, a scanner can save you keyboard time.

"If you have tons of documents that are in standard typeface and clearly typed in a large font you can save a lot of time by scanning," says Jann Jasper. "But in many situations you have to weigh the time you save by the time it takes you to scan everything that will keep filling up your hard drive. Not every one needs—or saves time—by scanning. I once timed how long it took me to type something against how long it took me to scan, including checking for errors and I didn't save any time."

HABITS & STRATEGIES

Use a virus scanning program. Some computer software packages come with a virus checker built right into the File Manager. If you don't have a program with a virus checker, install a commercial antivirus program to protect yourself and save the time of dealing with computer viruses that produce undesirable, untimely, and damaging messages and erasures.

Tape Recorders and Dictating Equipment

You can maximize your productive time while you're away from your desk by using a miniature tape recorder or portable pocket dictator to record your thoughts through verbal notes and dictate ideas, memos, and letters.

You can also use your tape recorder to save the time and expense of a long phone call to a colleague. When you have downtime, record what you want to communicate, send the cassette to the colleague, and ask him or her to respond by recording on the other side of the tape and getting it back to you.

Headsets

If your work necessitates being on the phone a great deal of the time, a headset will help you save time by freeing your hands to carry out other tasks while you talk on the phone. Among other things, you can file, open mail, sort papers, work at your computer, and send a fax. You can stand up and stretch and, almost best of all, you won't have to cradle the phone on your neck or grip the phone with your hand.

Financial Management Programs

These software programs automate your financial records and keep your income and expenses organized quickly and easily. They perform the following tasks:

- Track where your money goes
- Categorize your financial transactions
- Indicate current bank balances
- Help you stay on top of savings and investments
- Print checks and invoices
- Enable you to do electronic bill paying
- Coordinate tax information

Backup Systems

Few things can derail you as badly as losing material from your hard drive, whether it's from a computer crash or it's the shock of seeing a blank screen when you open an in-progress file and discover that, for one reason or another, you mistakenly closed the file before saving it and backing it up. Without the file on either your hard drive or a floppy disk, you lose irreplaceable amounts of time recovering and reinstalling material. Consequently, backing up your work is a huge time-saver compared to having to do it over.

To avoid crashes and catastrophes make sure you have a good backup system. Make equally sure to attach a Post-it-size sign saying, "Back up, back up, back up" near your computer screen to remind you to use it. Back up everything on your hard drive once a month and your day's work at the end of each day. For big projects, play it even safer by backing up material at interim times throughout the day.

Use a felt-tipped pen to mark your floppies with color-coded labels. This will provide fast and easy identification. Keep extra sets of backup floppies in a site away from your office so you'll have them in case of fire or another disaster. You may want to add the double-double protection of printing out hard copies of your most important work.

Computer Plus Paper: A Practical Choice for the Multitudes

"There's a marriage between computer and paper."
Debbie Gilster, small business consultant and owner of Organize & Computerize

Though we can't—and don't want to—escape technology, there are still a sizable number of us who haven't abandoned paper entirely for some of our daily tasks. In fact, in my talks with busy people, I've found a great majority work with a combination of computer-plus-paper systems.

For instance, Debbie Gilster, who uses a contact manager, does not use the calendar system in it because she's in clients' offices most of the time and finds a paper calendar works best for her.

"When I'm with a client and want to reschedule an appointment all my personal and business commitments are right there with me on my calendar," she said. "I can set up whatever needs to be done quickly. Then when I get back to the office it's all in place on my paper calendar so it's double duty for me to reenter that information in the computer. My life is on my paper calendar."

To use a combination of computer plus paper successfully, here are four dos:

Do record *everything* on your on-paper planner and calendar if a paper system works better for you than putting your whole life on a full contact manager or electronic organizer.

Do set up computer files, disks, and directories with the same headings as your paper files.

"Classify everything into major categories first," explains Donna McMillan. "Then, since we're all visual and accustomed to working with paper, do the physical organizing of your paper files. After that create computer files that match the paper files. For instance, I have a paper file in my file drawer called 'Business Promo' and a file on my computer directory with the same name."

CAUTION

Don't be too quick to delete a program that comes packaged with your computer—if you think you may not need or want it. Sometimes programs work together, so stop! before you delete.

Do consider using the day's date, including the year, as part of the file name on your computer directory. Say you spend a Thursday drafting a report on a conference. Use Thursday's date on your file name. If you write a different version of the same document at a later time, name that file with that day's date. When you call up your files you know when each was created and can open the one you want quickly. Be sure to also put the date on your printout matching paper files before you put them in your file cabinet.

Do maintain both your computer and paper files by keeping them up to date. Get rid of papers you no longer need and delete the matching files from your hard drive. Occasionally, something may fall through the cracks with this not-saving-everything system. But as Jann Jasper puts it, "You can't treat every piece of paper as though it is one of Moses' tablets from the mount."

MINUTES MATTER

"If you can't find something in 30 seconds it's in the wrong place."
Donna McMillan, founder of McMillan &
Company Professional Organizing

How Can You Identify When and How Technology Will Be a Time-Saver for You?

If you're uncertain about *when* and *how* new or upgraded technology and programs will help you manage time, follow these three steps.

STEP BY STEP

Step 1: Consult with a computer guru who's familiar with your business needs. This can be a friend or professional, but do get his or her input. Ask about the pros and cons of the products you're considering and whether or not the programs are likely to

Be right for you and your needs

Save you time

Make you more productive

Enhance your value in the workplace

If you're truly a beginner in Hi-Tech Land, the programs that come with computers are the right things to start with. The value of the word processing program—as opposed to typing—is immediately incontestable.

When you're ready to upgrade, you may want some kind of contact manager or electronic organizer, along with some of the other products mentioned in this chapter.

Step 2: Fill out this evaluation before you go to the computer store, take it with you when you go, and talk with a knowledgeable salesperson about it.

What tasks do I need to do in my work? _____

_____

What are my present ways of doing these tasks? _____

_____

What do I need and want to change to accomplish more than I do in my present way of doing things? _____

_____

How and *when* would the purchase of some state-of-the-art computer and hi-tech equipment help me make these changes? _____

_____

What special features do I want and need? _____

_____

Will those features and equipment be easy and convenient for me to use?

_____

Will I like the product and program and be comfortable with it? _____

_____

Step 3: Take time to learn your way around the basics. Unless you're technology-oriented and understand immediately how to use electronic products, plan on devoting a good chunk of time to learning the necessary skills. It can't be emphasized enough that with each technological upgrade, the time you spend becoming proficient will pay dividends later on.

HABITS & STRATEGIES

Cultivate a friendly relationship with an employee at the computer supply store with which you do business. Get to know this ally well and keep him or her up to date on what functions you need from your hardware, software, and electronic products. Shop at the store only when your user-friendly contact is scheduled to work. A quick phone call to the store let's you know your helper's hours and prevents wasting time on a shopping trip in which you won't have personalized support.

CAUTION

Read *the manuals and* use *the tutorials that come with your hi-tech equipment.*

Not all of us can teach ourselves, so, if after reading the manuals and tutorials, you need extra help, save yourself time by going to a class or hiring a computer consultant. Then practice, practice, practice.

MINUTES MATTER

Use the print preview, spellcheck and thesaurus functions in your software programs. They're big minute savers.

Whatever you do, don't hold off going with today's technological flow. Find the *right* programs and products for *you*—and constantly remind yourself you don't need everything. When you go for whatever is on the market, you clutter your time and space with products and programs you don't need and probably won't ever use.

Always remember the main thing is to concentrate on the whens and hows that will move *you* ahead in time-saving ways and put you on the right track. Above all, keep things simple. That's the bottom line.

"Out of clutter, find simplicity."
Albert Einstein

For Further Information

The following list of products and resources is a short recap of the products most commonly used by the wide range of people I spoke to about their use of technology. In addition, I have listed some books that can offer you a more in-depth look at the Internet and its benefits. For an in-person review of products and prices, and personal assistance and demonstrations, visit your computer supply store.

Hardware
Electronic Organizers/PIMs/PDAs

HP 300 Series Palmtop PCs *US ROBOTICS PalmPilot Personal*
SHARP Zaurus *H&R BLOCK Names & Dates*

Software
Contact Managers ### *Financial Planning*

ACT! Contact Management Program *QUICKEN and QUICK BOOKS*
ECCO PRO Contact Management Program

Virus Protection
Norton Anti-Virus Software

Commercial Online Services and Internet Browsers

America Online *CompuServe*
Microsoft Net *Netscape*

Books

The Internet for Busy People The World Wide Web
Christian Crumish, Complete Reference
Osborn/McGraw Hill *Rick Stout, Osborn/McGraw-Hill*

The Internet Yellow Pages 3e The Internet Science, Research &
Harley Hahn, Osborn/McGraw-Hill Technology
Rich Stout and Morgan Davis,
Osborn/McGraw-Hill

Net Law: The Internet
Your Rights in the Online World Complete Reference 2e
Lance Rose, Osborn/McGraw-Hill *Harley Hahn,*
Osborn/McGraw-Hill

Checkpoints

You have thought about the available hardware and software that might give you an edge in winning the time-gaining race.

You have determined whether or not a computerized contact manager will provide the time-saving benefits you seek.

You have considered the worth of a portable electronic organizer as a part of your overall time management strategy.

You know the time-saving value of a fax/modem integrated with your computer to facilitate your communications.

You have gone online and begun your exploration of the vast benefits of the Web.

You have remembered to back up all of your files on your hard disk and will continue to protect each day's work with a backup file.

You have found the appropriate balance for you between paper and electronic organization.

You have evaluated your technological needs carefully and lined up a knowledgeable computer professional to help you upgrade and implement potential new systems.

In the next chapter, you will see how to stay on your time track through decision making, delegating, and saying "no" instead of an unnecessary "yes."

Decide, Delegate, and *Do* Say "No"

INCLUDES

- Complementing your time management skills with decision making know-how

- Learning to delegate tasks to others who perform acceptably to free yourself for higher-valutized projects

- Understanding the wisdom of saying "no" to time-consuming and unnecessary distractions

FAST FORWARD

Bolster Decision Making Skills ➤ *pp. 98–100*

- Avoid roadblocks to making decisions by knowing what is expected and gathering sufficient information to make a sound determination—then do it.
- Evaluate why a decision is needed and the pros and cons of the different choices you might make.

Time-Saving Tips for Making Decisions ➤ *pp. 100–101*

- Set decision deadlines—especially the small ones involved in larger projects—to get yourself moving forward.
- Proceed with confidence once your decision is made, remembering that options can always be refined as you progress.

Learn to Delegate ➤ *pp. 101–103*

- Realize that teamwork is one of the great time-savers.
- Create a weekly worksheet delineating all jobs to be accomplished and the team available to help you complete them.
- Determine what tasks only you can do, distribute work to others with clear directions and expectations, and then let them do it.
- Give your team members their own deadlines for completing assigned work.
- Schedule brief meetings with your group to monitor progress and answer questions.
- Resist the temptation to discuss details of your team's work with them until the job is completed.

Say "No" to Unnecessary Requests ➤ *pp. 104–106*

- Ponder the experiences of others who always say "yes" and reflect on how your own life and time is affected by your "yes" choices.
- Rate your ability to say "no" when you should (and your expertise in saying it) so that it will be accepted and respected by others.

Now that you're on the main line with computer and hi-tech streamliners, the next components for staying on track are deciding, delegating, and saying "no" (instead of an unnecessary "yes").

As the clock ticks off the minutes, the way to gain the most benefits from these three components is to realize the following:

- You can't wipe out all risks by postponing decisions, since no decisions are entirely risk-free.
- You don't have to do everything yourself when someone with fewer time demands than you could do the task adequately.
- You're practical and responsible when you say "no," without any guilt, to unnecessary commitments.

Once you put these components into action, they'll turn your time-managed life around.

Decision Making Skills Are Junior Partners to Your Time Management Skills

You lose time—and gain tension—when you put off making decisions for significant lengths of time. Besides, delays are seldom useful in improving the quality of your decision.

Naturally, it's savvy to take enough time to think through issues before you move on them. But too often, while we do this, we're stopped in our tracks by roadblocks.

Four Roadblocks and Four Start-ups

Roadblock	Start-up
You're afraid you'll make a mistake.	No one is right all the time. Be willing to take some chances.
You think you need more information to make an appropriate decision.	Gather sufficient information to make sound decisions. But don't feel you must dig up all possible information. If additional facts are not apt to affect the outcome to any great degree, know when to stop and manage with what you have.
You're unsure of how to proceed.	Clarify what's expected of you and get complete and specific instructions about the project or issue that requires a decision.
You're anxious about the consequences, i.e., you might hurt someone or turn someone against you.	It's human to be distressed over this, but it's also inevitable that every decision can't always be satisfying to everyone. You have to be strong and not waiver when it's the right decision.

HABITS & STRATEGIES

Holding back on making decisions while you gather more facts than you need is a tremendous time-waster and often the path of least resistance to moving ahead on actions you'll eventually have to take.

Five Important Things to Remember to Avoid Losing Time

1. Set deadlines for making decisions.

2. Decide quickly on low-level choices without agonizing over each one.

Decision Making Worksheet

Since competence in making decisions is a major factor in managing your time, the following worksheet can help you take an objective look at the issues involved in decisions. Use all the lines you need.

Why is this decision needed? _____

_____

What will be the positive results of making this decision? _____

_____

What could be the negative consequences? _____

_____

What are all the possible decisions I could make? _____

_____

What are the alternatives to these potentials? _____

_____

How effective would these options be? _____

_____

Improved decision making skills don't happen overnight. But when you make it a regular practice to evaluate all the issues and move in the right direction, you'll gradually upgrade your abilities and save yourself valuable time.

HABITS & STRATEGIES

Never underestimate the power of intuition when you're faced with making decisions.

3. Avoid procrastinating on big decisions by making a small decision about some aspect of the overall project or issue. This will get you started rather than hold you back for too long while you worry about all the details.

4. Have confidence in your own judgment to act on a decision once you've concluded what's the best right decision.

5. Remember that even when you make the right decision, every decision won't be perfect. But at least you've been decisive and taken steps to move ahead.

HABITS & STRATEGIES

When you make an important decision—especially if it's one you've wrestled with—write the decision concisely on a small index card and put it in your wallet. Read it frequently to reinforce the importance of the decision and to keep you focused on the follow-up.

Delegating Is a Skill That Gains Time

The best use of your time often means asking for help and, when you feel overwhelmed, delegating some tasks to assistants or other supportive people, if you're fortunate enough to have them.

Rather than doing routine work that takes your time from must-dos and should-dos, have enough confidence in yourself and others to believe they can handle some of the work. Unfortunately, though, there are more roadblocks here that stop many people from delegating as much as they could or should.

Four Roadblocks and Four Start-ups

"Typically a number of tasks can be safely delegated. Routine tasks, work requiring a great deal of repetitious detail, jobs other people are better qualified to do, and tasks that don't require crucial decision making can all be delegated."
Odette Pollar, management and organization consultant

Roadblock	Start-up
You want to do everything yourself.	Force yourself to focus on tasks that *only* you can do and ask for help for some of the tasks people, besides you, could do.
You feel you can do a job better than anyone else.	Stop thinking you must give your hands-on attention to everything. Consider the positives and negatives of not getting a job done exactly as you would do it compared to not getting it completed at all.

You subscribe to the "it's easier to do it myself" syndrome

Let go! After you tell helpers what should be done and what to do, first relax and let them do things their way as long as the end results are what they should be.

You fear that if you relinquish a job to someone else you'll lose control and another person will get the credit you want.

Today is the era of teamwork. We need others to cover all bases and save all of us time. Control and credit must be shared for meaningful productivity.

Nine Important Things to Remember When You Delegate

1. "First of all, be sensitive to the feelings of the individual who gets the work dumped on him or her," advises a business friend who describes himself as the person to whom work gets delegated (and without someone to whom he can delegate the overflow). "To say 'Here, I need this by four o'clock but I'm too busy to do it' is rude and demeaning. It's like hearing 'My time is too valuable to do the work but yours is so worthless you can do it.' "

2. Match your expectations to your helpers' abilities.

3. Give them specific directions about what you expect of them.

4. Make it clear that you count on them to work on their own except for coming to you with necessary questions.

5. Ask them to hold questions that arise and come to you with questions in batches instead of taking everyone's time with one-by-one questions.

Delegating Worksheet

The following worksheet can help you take an objective look at when and how you can ask for help and free yourself to go forward with the high-value jobs you must do yourself. Give yourself all the space you need to answer each question fully.

Write down the tasks that come to your desk in one week's time. _____
_____

Assign a 1, 2, 3, 4, 5 degree of importance to each one. _____
_____

List which of the 4 and 5 tasks could be delegated to someone else. _____
_____

Indicate the person or persons who could handle those tasks. _____
_____

Mark by each person's name the exact task you want done, along with how you want it done.

Helper   Task   How it should be done
_____
_____
_____
_____
_____

6. Establish a due date for when you anticipate delegated work to be returned to you and put that date on your calendar.

7. Monitor the tasks you delegate and check with your helpers periodically to see how they're doing. At the same time, allow them to carry a job through to completion without hanging on to every detail and checking on them excessively once they understand what to do.

8. Keep on top of what you delegate so that if something happens to the person to whom you delegated work, you don't lose time reassembling the task.

9. Give people feedback when their job is finished and credit them for what they did when credit is due.

Do Say "No"

Naturally, you must say "yes" to the significant and legitimate requirements that are expected of you—*and this makes it even more vital to say "no" to unnecessary requests, both in and out of work.*

The inability to do this is another time management roadblock, and when you say "yes" to excessive demands, you lose your grip on important commitments and find yourself in a tangled web, caught up in too many directions at once.

HABITS & STRATEGIES

Delegating may be hard at first, but it's a time-wise decision for achieving time management goals.

A Never-Say-No Lawyer's Story

A new lawyer in a suburban town was told by a lawyer-mentor that the way to establish and build his practice was to get his finger in the pot of many community activities. The lawyer took that advice to heart, and within two years of setting up shop, he was practicing law six days a week (some of it pro bono) to meet the call for his services.

He spent the away-from-work hours he had serving on the town council, working on a hospital fund drive, chairing a "Save the Environment" task force, and saying "I'll get back to you" whenever people asked him to assume other obligations. When he said "yes" to the presidency of his church's administrative board, his wife announced she was moving out and separating from him.

"I married *you*," she told him, "not Mr. Community Leader!"

CAUTION

Saying "yes" to every request that comes across the board equates saying "no" to hours and minutes you want or need for yourself.

A Never-Say-No Editor's Story

A magazine editor began her career with an assistant's job after graduating from college with a journalism major and a minor in nutrition. She worked in various capacities while she kept her eye on the food editor's job as her ultimate goal. She married and had three children in her first five years of working, and as her home life grew busier, her work life expanded, too. Among the things she said "yes" to was a freelance job doing reviews for the magazine's movie page.

That job involved afterwork screenings, so her days grew longer and longer. They started with driving her baby to the sitter's, leaving her two-year-old at day care, and taking her son to his kindergarten class—for which she'd said "yes" to being class mother. At night she dragged herself back home, just in time to tuck in the children after her husband picked them up and gave them their evening meal.

She was so creative in developing the magazine's movie page her editor asked her to do a food column, too. Of course, she said "yes" to this minigoal of moving to the food pages, and when she was offered the unexpected chance to be the assistant food editor she said "yes" to that.

But when it was time for the ultimate "yes"—when the magazine's food editor retired and she was tagged for the job—she shocked everyone with a "no" to the job that had been her goal.

"Although I'd always wanted this, I'd suddenly reached a point where I was burned out, swamped, and resentful about all I had to do," she admitted. "I was going in so many directions I didn't know where I was *at*. But miraculously I *did* know that the time commitments that went with this promotion were not for me at this time.

"Along with saying 'no' to the job, I gave up going to the office and doing the movie page. Instead I arranged to work at home and now I do the food column from there and write food articles for a supplement each year. This gives me time for both work and home—and, believe me, I've learned how to say 'no' to all other unnecessary demands."

MINUTES MATTER

Watch out for "I'll get back to you" if it only delays the "No" you should say.

Worksheet to Determine How Effective You Are at Saying "No" to Unnecessary Demands

Rate yourself on how you say "no" in the following test. Mark A for usually, B *for* sometimes, *and* C *for* never.

_____ Do you take a good look at your schedule and current time commitments before assuming additional responsibilities?

_____ Do you refrain from adding new commitments and responsibilities without subtracting something else?

_____ Do you consider the time costs of not saying "no" and then count to 10 before saying "yes?"

_____ Do you say "no" immediately when you should say it—without losing time worrying about saying it?

_____ Do you practice ahead of time how to say "no" politely and firmly to a variety of requests?

_____ Do you have a stock explanation for your "no," such as "I have a conflict," "I'm sorry I can't do it because—," or "I can't do it within that time frame," so people will respect your "no?"

_____ Do you point out to the person assigning new tasks what you already have to do and ask what he or she wants you to eliminate to make room for the new task?

_____ Do you suggest, when appropriate, that someone else with less to do at the moment might be more appropriate for the task?

Scoring

Mostly *A* Answers: *You're better than the average person in saying "no" instead of "yes."*
Primarily *B* Answers: *You do a middle-of-the-road job but there's room for improvement.*
Chiefly *C* Answers: *You're selling yourself short by not saying "no" enough.*

You'll never satisfy everyone with your "nos," decisions, or delegations, so don't waste time on false obligations and a fear of displeasing others. Acknowledge, instead, that this trio will help you improve your productivity at work and provide you with time to devote yourself to your other goals and values, too.

MINUTES MATTER

The shortest minute-saving word is no.

Checkpoints

You have uncovered the hurdles that keep you from making effective decisions in a timely manner.

You have chosen how to set timetables for making decisions and, then, how to move forward with confidence.

You have determined the ways in which a team effort can most efficiently get your objectives accomplished and then followed up with delegating work accordingly.

You have learned how to say "no" to activities and projects that sidetrack you and delay your progress in realizing highly valutized goals.

In the next chapter, you will see how to do your best in managing time when bad things happen to good time schedules.

When Bad Things Happen to Good Time Schedules

INCLUDES

- Avoiding time crushers at work that alter your carefully scheduled plans

- Identifying ways to keep personal time crushers under control

- Anticipating the time-crushing drawbacks of equipment failure

- Learning to discourage unwanted and unneeded interruptions

- Planning for participation in or scheduling of effective and time-sensitive meetings

- Communicating efficiently and adeptly by telephone

FAST FORWARD

Work Time Crushers ➤ pp. 113–116

- Discuss the daily work already on your plate before agreeing to an emergency job—and together with your boss, valutize the new work before redoing your schedule.
- Help team members get and stay on track when their work is essential to the completion of your project.
- Schedule one-on-one meetings in *your* office so you can move quickly on to other tasks in the eventuality of late or no-show appointments.
- Keep your higher-ups regularly informed in writing about the number, complexity, and status of projects you are currently working on so they can effectively evaluate the benefits or risks of giving you new assignments.
- Offer alternative solutions for completing tasks for which you simply must say "no."

Home Time Crushers ➤ pp. 116–118

- *Preplan* for child care emergencies by enlisting the support of your spouse, family, friends, and sitters who can fill in for you until you can readjust your schedule.
- Prepare what-to-do lists for your family, friends, or neighbors in case of emergencies such as illness, accidents, fire, and so on, including all relevant phone numbers, so that quick action can be taken even while you are enroute to deal with the crisis yourself.
- Ease the tension of out-of-control times, such as a death in your family, by understanding that coworkers will be supportive and that, although you may be out of sync for a while, you will be able to return to normal patterns.
- Don't compound the problems of emotionally draining periods in your personal life by beating up on yourself for missing the mark on time management.

Equipment Time Crushers ➤ *pp. 118–120*

- Learn how to correct common printer, computer hardware and software, and copier problems.
- Anticipate the possibility of breakdowns and keep duplicate items at the ready, such as tape recorders, batteries, and extension cords, whenever possible.
- Have a backup plan that does not involve equipment, such as a flip chart for a presentation when the overhead projector doesn't arrive, to make sure that you can follow through on your objectives, no matter what.

Excessive Interruption Time Crushers ➤ *pp. 120–122*

- Be aware of the types of colleagues who cause needless interruptions during your day, such as gossips, complainers, or advice seekers.
- Discourage unwanted visitors by closing your door or being direct in telling them you don't have time to talk.
- Set aside a certain time each day for an open office hour and let coworkers know that you welcome them at this time and no other unless you have a prescheduled appointment with them.

Excessive Meeting Time Crushers ➤ *pp. 122–125*

- Find out the agenda for each meeting you're requested to attend and determine in advance whether or not your presence is really necessary.
- Apply a time frame to each item on your agenda when you schedule meetings, communicate this information to all participants, and stick to it during the meeting.
- Invite only the participants who need to be at any meeting you convene. This limits the possibilities of getting sidetracked because of too many contributors.

- Arrive at meetings on time, not early or late, and if you are in charge, begin all meetings on time.
- Have a real reason to excuse yourself from meetings that exceed the agreed upon time limit for that meeting.

Excessive Phone Call Time Crushers ➤ pp. 125–128

- Use an answering machine or voice mail to screen calls or take messages.
- Respond to messages left for you as promptly as possible—don't be one of those whose credibility is hurt because you are always apologizing for taking so long to get back in touch.
- Encourage family and friends to minimize or eliminate their calls to you during your working hours.
- Know what you want a phone call to accomplish before you make one. Then get right to the point.
- Tell a caller up front just how much time you have to speak at the moment and, if necessary, reschedule the call for a convenient time for both of you.
- Develop the skill of ending phone conversations quickly and graciously.

You have your morning planned perfectly with a good fix on your time. Your workplace and papers are in a manageable state. Your computer is turned on. By 10 A.M. you've made a decision and delegated a job. You've also said "no" to a lunch invitation. You're at full throttle for the day.

But wait! Your boss approaches you with a rush job for a client. The client is difficult, to say the least—and he wants the job yesterday. Now there's a danger of losing him if your office doesn't come through. The emergency flasher and warning signs blink, and before you can blink yourself your own planned day is as obsolete at your client's yesterday.

Because of our interdependencies, this scenario is familiar, since bad things happen to good timetables to everyone everywhere. No one can *ever* completely control all of the people and events that crash and crush our time.

Fortunately, though, there are what-to-dos that will control to some degree the major time crushers.

Five Common Work Time Crushers

Time Crusher 1

You're already overwhelmed with work when you're faced with the same kind of rush job mentioned at the start of this chapter. This time, it's a boss who announces a speaking engagement at a sales conference and needs to include sales figures for the past five years. Your boss demands that you do an analysis for the conference before you do anything else.

What to Do

With an ultimatum like this from your boss, you have little choice but to say good-bye to your planned time schedule and, then, go back and re-create another plan for your day. Before you acquiesce, however, you might spell out to your boss all that you have to get done that day that he or she has already assigned and ask what should be eliminated so you can do the additional work. Sometimes when bosses see how much you're already doing for them they may say the rush job can wait a day—and you will buy yourself time.

If this doesn't work, the next best thing is to accept the need to shift your time management around without getting stressed out about it. Address the unanticipated setback and work through that (and your other work) in the most effective, efficient way you can, given the time constrictions in which you have to work.

On the other hand, if a coworker rather than the boss is pushing the panic button, stand firm. Instead of being too quick to shift your time schedule, try something like, "I'm interested in this project, and I'll give you the input I can. But I can't do it today."

HABITS & STRATEGIES

Anticipate crises and have ready-to-go contingency plans. Naturally, you can't have contingency plans for everything. But you should have them for critical situations so you'll be able to act quickly without losing time having to think about it.

Time Crusher 2

You need a report from a coworker to continue on a deadline job. You've anticipated receiving it, but now the coworker disappoints you by not coming through. This traps you in a time crunch. You're at a loss about what to do.

What to Do

The right way to make the best use of your time in this kind of situation is to get to work with the material you already have and leave empty spaces for the information you still need from your coworker. While you do this, make your disappointment clear and emphasize that getting the material *now* is critical. Monitor the person from whom you need the input to be sure it's in the works.

Time Crusher 3

You have a 12 P.M. lunch appointment to go over a joint project with a colleague from a branch office. By 12:30, he's a no-show, and you're cooling your heels in the restaurant wasting time you can't afford to lose.

What to Do

Make a phone call to find out where the colleague is. If there's no answer (or an answer that he's on his way) allow yourself just so much more time to wait. If he still doesn't show, order a quick lunch and get on your way and on schedule for whatever your next commitment is. Leave word for him that you've gone in case he shows, and make a mental note to have him come to *your* office for future appointments so there'll be no waiting time to waste.

Time Crusher 4

Your work is ballooning because your company is downsizing and not hiring replacements when employees leave. As the work is divided among the remaining employees, you've been given so many additional jobs you don't have time to do your own work as adequately as you'd like to.

What to Do

When top echelon starts distributing duties, speak up right away in a non-complaining manner with such phrases as "I feel I should mention upfront that I'm already bogged down with other urgent jobs right now. Here's what I'm doing." Then in a very specific way—and in writing—make the company aware of your current responsibilities and the time it takes to do each job in the way it should be done.

This probably won't get you completely home free from all additional duties. But it may get rid of some of them and, as you work accordingly, it will help cut down on some of the frustration of not being able to balance your time exactly as you want to.

Time Crusher 5

You're asked to work late or take a client to dinner, and there's no way you can do this on that particular day.

What to Do

Offer to take the work home and point out you'll be only a telephone call away. Another potential is to say you'll come in early the next morning and work on whatever needs to be done first thing. If the issue involves taking a client to dinner, explain why you can't do it and suggest someone else who might play host. Most clients will understand—even if your boss is disenchanted at first.

Four Common Home Time Crushers

Time Crusher 1

You're have a child-care emergency. The school is unexpectedly closed. The nanny calls in sick. Your son wakes up with a fever. You're held up at work and your daycare closes at 6 P.M.

What to Do

Always have alternative child-care arrangements ready to be set up at a moment's notice. Compile an on-call support list with phone numbers of family members, teenage or older sitters, and neighbors or friends who will come to your rescue. Also make arrangements with your spouse or mate to take over for each other in emergencies.

Time Crusher 2

You get a call from your elderly mother's neighbor who, when she stopped for a visit, discovered your mother had fallen. The neighbor thinks she broke her

"Little minds are tamed and subdued by misfortunes. Great minds rise above them."
Washington Irving

arm and they're both hysterical. The neighbor doesn't know what doctor to call and, since she doesn't drive, she can't take your mother to the hospital emergency room. She needs you to tell her what to do—and both she and your mother want you to come to your mother's house right away.

What to Do

Though you'll probably have to leave work and go to your mother's immediately this time, you won't have to drop everything in the future and leave before you can turn around if you plan ahead with a clear what-to-do for these family-circle emergencies.

You can save time—and get things started without you when emergencies happen—if, as part of your what-to-do list, you post by the phone in your home, at work, and at the home of any family member or friend for whom you're responsible (1) your work number, (2) doctors' numbers, (3) your spouse or mate's work number, (4) a number or numbers for other family members, (5) the police department's number (an officer will call the paramedics, ambulance, or fire department if necessary).

It's also a good idea to see that all of your children's schools have this list, too. With this kind of preparation, time can be saved and help can be set in motion before you're in a position to take over yourself.

Time Crusher 3

You're confronted with an all-consuming family crisis (rather than a short-term one like the broken arm). This time it may be a chronic accident or injury, a long-term illness, or the death of a loved one. These misfortunes take their toll on you, and it's hard to control your time as you ordinarily do.

What to Do

No one is immune to these out-of-control times when life and time are out of balance. It's hard to continue as usual, too, so you may have to modify some aspects of the way you manage your time and, due to your circumstances, temporarily change the manner in which you do some things.

It helps in these times of misfortune to live by the attitude and philosophy that nothing is forever, while you do the best you can. But if, when you are in control of your time, you give your all to managing it well, most of the people with whom you work will be supportive of the times when you can't.

Time Crusher 4

You may have a personal crisis, as opposed to a family crisis, and you're not managing your time very well because of a health problem, extreme fatigue, relationship turning point, or other misfortune. You know you've back-tracked in handling your time, but you seem to have no spirit to do anything right now.

What to Do

You're human, so there will be back-track times when you *don't* feel like managing your time because of bad things in your personal life. But your dampened spirits concerning time management and the problem that's absorbing you will eventually pass—as everything does.

In the meantime, give yourself a break and refuse to add discouragement about time management to the other problem you're experiencing. Once your life comes together, your time management motivation will improve, too.

Three Common Equipment Time Crushers

Time Crusher 1

You have 15 minutes to print a report in order to meet your deadline. But when you turn on your printer, you get a paper jam. You're successful in getting the paper released, but then the printer won't print.

What to Do

Computers, software, printers, copiers, and fax machines are notorious for acting up and holding you back just when you need them most. Sometimes the problem is a minimal one and needn't be a time-waster if you learn how to change a printer or copier cartridge and work around software glitches that happen periodically. In addition to saving time by knowing how to fix minor problems yourself, do preventive maintenance on your equipment to avoid foul-ups at critical times.

Time Crusher 2

You're scheduled to give a presentation and the audio/video tape or overhead projector doesn't start up when you're ready to begin. While you SOS the maintenance department, you lose time getting your show on the road (and maybe the audience's attention, too.)

Work/Home/Equipment Worksheet

If you're challenged with repeated bad things such as the foregoing common ones, this worksheet will help you evaluate when and why these time crushers happen. Use all the space you need. There's obviously no scoring involved. The answers are strictly for you.

What type of bad things do I experience most often? _____

_____

_____

Are these happenings caused by something I did or didn't do?_____

_____

_____

What did I do wrong if I was at fault? _____

_____

_____

What did someone else do wrong that we might talk about and work through together?_____

_____

_____

What have I done in the past to solve comparable bad happenings?_____

_____

_____

What to Do

Be like the Boy Scouts—be prepared. Always have on hand two sets of audiovisual items plus extra bulbs, extension cords, and wall plugs. Also carry extra batteries for tape recorders and wireless microphones with you.

Time Crusher 3

Your tape recorder didn't pick up everything you expected it would while you took notes at a meeting. When you played it back, there were lapses, and now you're without important information you need to complete a conference report.

What to Do

Stop depending exclusively on your tape recorder. Take sketchy notes as a backup. While your recorder is on and you're jotting down your backup notes, see that the timer on your recorder is set at zero when the tape begins. When something you want to be sure to include in a report is said, write in the margin of your notes where your timer is. Then, when you're writing your report or whatever, you can go back to that spot quickly. This saves you the time of listening to the whole tape and transcribing material you may not need.

Excessive Interruption Time Crushers

Normal interruptions are part of your job, so, as pointed out in Chap. 1, you can't get rid of all of them—nor would you really want to. You have to adopt the attitude that some are not excessive and rightfully require your time.

But there's a difference between this kind and the *excessive* office interruptions that, if you fail to control them, do bad things to your day. In a phone interview, Dr. Donald R. Gallagher, a time management authority and former research director and co-owner of *communications briefings,* cited the following types of coworkers as the most common cause of office interruptions:

Social butterflies.   They go from one place to another, updating and gabbing.

Office politicians.   They think you can help them or they're "buttering you up."

Advice seekers. They say, "What would you do in my position?"

Gossipers. They play on a weakness in human nature.

I-don't-have-enough-to-doers. They tell you how much they are over-worked.

You-should-be-as-sick-as-I-am interrupters. They've had—or are sure they are getting—whatever physical malady is featured in the popular press.

Complainers. They love to tell you what's wrong with the world, humanity, the economy, the in-laws, and the office.

MINUTES MATTER

Sidestep internal interruptions by disciplining yourself to stick to the task at hand without hopping up every few minutes to check out something else.

You can keep these and other excesses in check and control your time better with the following suggestions:

- Evaluate the importance of interruptions
- Consider whether they must be dealt with immediately, no matter what your schedule is
- Determine when and how they can be scheduled for another time
- Plan ahead on how they can be eliminated or diverted to someone else

"Ask interrupters if they're feeling all right (if nothing else works). They'll get concerned and rush to the nearest mirror to see what they look like."
Dr. Donald Gallagher, time management authority in communications briefings

Nine More What-To-Dos to Control Excessive Interruptions

1. Discourage spur-of-the-moment visitors by encouraging people to make appointments with you to save their time and yours.

2. Place your desk in an area where people can't see you through the door. If you can do this, interrupters will be less likely to come in.

3. Close your door (if you have one) when your sixth sense tells you an unnecessary interruption is on the way.

4. Remove extra chairs from your office (or put papers on the chairs) if your door is open. People won't stay as long if they come in and have to stand.

5. Avoid people coming in, whenever possible, by meeting interrupters at the door (and appearing to be leaving your office) when you see them coming.

6. Tell interrupters you're busy and that, except for a real urgency, you can't talk at the moment.

7. Glance at your watch every few minutes if people don't move on.

8. Suggest *your* time frame for handling staff questions and other interruptions if they *are* an urgency. Say something like, "I'll be free at 11:30." Then arrange to meet people at their workplace. In that way, you can keep the interruption short and control when to leave.

9. Get back to the task you were doing as soon as possible after interruptions.

MINUTES MATTER

Research shows that, after an interruption, it takes four to five minutes to get back up to speed on what you were doing before the interruption.

Excessive Meeting Time Crushers

Meetings are expensive in terms of time, and when you're trapped in extraneous ones, you're destined to trash a good deal of your day sitting through repetitive discussions.

Unfortunately, meetings your boss sets up may be command performances and, regardless of how unnecessary they are, you may have to say good-bye to the time you could use to better advantage. Fortunately, though, you have better control when a colleague arranges a meeting or when you yourself are responsible for getting people together.

In the case of a colleague calling the meeting, you can frequently control whether or not to attend by finding out what the purpose of the meeting is and asking for specifics on the agenda. If you see your attendance isn't at stake, bow out of as many of these meetings as you can. On the other hand, when you're in charge (either because you want to set up a meeting or are asked to organize one), there are time-saving, controlling measures you can take.

Obviously, the first one is to answer the question "Is this meeting necessary?" If the answer is "no" forget it. If it's "yes," consider alternatives to taking your own and other people's time for an inhouse meeting. Here are four alternatives.

- Send e-mail requests to prospective attendees providing information and asking for input on what would be covered at the meeting
- Prepare a memo to pass on the information after you obtain and compile it
- Set up a telephone conference call
- Arrange a breakfast or lunch get-together to discuss the issue during nonworking time

If you have to have an inhouse meeting, invite only people who have (1) hands-on knowledge of the topic at hand, (2) essential input to contribute, and (3) the authority to make decisions and take responsible actions. Limit the number of attendees because the meeting will take less time with fewer people engaged in discussions.

When possible, group meetings together—either all in the morning or all in the afternoon. To avoid breaking up primary work hours, aim for 8 A.M. meetings, before-lunch meetings, and end-of-the-day meetings when, rather than stretching out a meeting, people will be concerned with leaving for the day. Finally, if you're in a position to do it, encourage your place of business to set up a policy where at least one day a week is free of meetings.

CAUTION

Is this meeting necessary?

Eleven More What-To-Dos to Cut Down on Wasting-Time Meetings
If You're Running a Meeting

1. Hold your meeting in a conference room or somewhere other than your office. When it's not in your office, you can leave as soon as the meeting is over. When it's at your place, however, you can be stuck with people who want to stay on and take extra time talking to you about the meeting.

2. Let attendees know the purpose of the meeting *prior* to the meeting.

3. Start on time.

4. Evaluate the worth of each item on your agenda and set a time frame and limit for each item, depending on its importance.

5. Stick to your important points (preferably no more than three or four) and don't get sidetracked.

6. Refrain from wasting time hassling over an item that comes up on which no one has adequate information. Instead, appoint an ad hoc committee to find out more about it.

7. Let attendees know they have just so much time to cover the agenda.

8. Wear an alarm wrist watch set to go off at the time the meeting should end. Use it as a signal for everyone to move on.

HABITS & STRATEGIES

Pass out copies of your meeting agenda ahead of time. In addition to noting the topics to be covered, frame the topics as questions. For example, if "House and Grounds Maintenance" is on the agenda, ask the question, "What steps do we need to take to improve the system?" When attendees come prepared with specific answers to specific questions, meetings move faster.

If You're Attending a Meeting

9. Plan to arrive when you know the meeting will be actually starting— and not one minute before. This will avoid wasting minutes waiting to begin or sitting through time-consuming preliminaries.

10. Stay at a meeting only as long as you're needed.

11. Schedule an appointment or incoming phone call for the ending time of the meeting so you'll have a good excuse to leave, should the meeting drag on.

HABITS & STRATEGIES

Follow up on meetings. Get minutes out promptly to all attendees and detail concisely (1) what actions were taken, (2) who was given the responsibility to pursue each action, and (3) when a progress report on the actions is due.

Excessive Phone Call Time Crushers

Undoubtedly, it's part of your job to spend some time on the phone, so you can't say a frustrated "oh, no" every time it rings. However, an infamous bad thing in anybody's schedule is too many phone calls we don't need to make or take.

As mentioned in Chap. 1, three primary ways to cut down on all kinds of time-taking phone calls is to do the following:

- Establish times when you make or take phone calls
- Use voice mail or an answering machine to record messages, screen calls, and help reduce calls you don't need or want to take
- Master the art of ending conversations quickly and graciously

It's even more vital to follow these guides when you're dealing with *excess* calls, so check yourself on your telephone time with the following questionnaire. Mark an *x* for your Yes or No answers and total them when you're done.

Telephone Questionnaire

		Yes	No
1.	Do you avoid staying on the phone when you could call back at a more convenient time?	___	___
2.	Do you call back as soon as your schedule permits it after getting a person's name and number?	___	___
3.	Do you save time by trying to return all of your callbacks at one time?	___	___
4.	Do you have an assistant screen and return calls for you—if you have an assistant?	___	___
5.	Do you give the assistant a list of people and family members to always put through or never put through?	___	___
6.	Do you ask your friends and family to minimize their calls to your workplace?	___	___
7.	Do you refrain from interrupting others by unimportant phone calls to them?	___	___
8.	Do you plan what you're going to say before you place a call?	___	___
9.	Do you get right to the point when you make or take calls?	___	___
10.	Do you keep papers you need to refer to by the phone when you make a call?	___	___
11.	Do you maintain notes about what transpired in important phone calls so you can check back on them without having to trust your memory?	___	___
	Total	___	___

Scoring: If most of your answers are Yes, give yourself a plus mark for the way you handle telephone time. If you have half Yes and half No answers, you're between a plus and a minus. If you've marked primarily No, you definitely need to zero in to improve time-saving telephone tactics.

"On the average, a phone call with a planned agenda takes seven minutes while an unplanned call takes twelve minutes. If you average just twelve calls per day, you can save yourself an hour with planned calls."
Stephanie Denton, professional organizer and teacher of time management techniques

CAUTION

Be selective about who gets the number for your mobile or car phones so the phones won't get jammed with calls. Be equally discriminating about the way you use these phones. You don't have to use them all the time just because you have an available phone. Relax a few moments at the health club (or wherever) without thinking you should get on the telephone.

Three More What-To-Dos to Decrease Excessive Phone Calls

1. Keep escape phrases to stop excessive calls before they start on the tip of your tongue. Try "I only have three minutes," "I'm on my way out," "I have someone in my office right now," "I have to get started on a project right away," and "I'm on a tight deadline and can't talk."

2. Let people to whom you leave messages on an answering machine know the best time to return your call so you won't be interrupted while you're busy. Similarly, ask callers to leave the number where they can be reached and the best time for you to call them back on your answering machine.

3. Ignore the ringing of the phone completely if you're *really* involved in a task that needs your full, uninterrupted attention. This will be okay sometimes. But, as a caveat to think about, too, my friend Jim Saelzler who has worked in a variety of capacities on various projects offers this view: "Bless people for not taking the approach 'I'm so important persons who have business to conduct with me can call me back if they need to.'

   "I'm really tired of dealing with people who will take care of business only on their own terms," he warned. "It's so exquisitely nice to work with someone who will respond to an issue, whatever it might be, quickly, directly, and efficiently.

   "That in itself may be one of the best time-saving tips for all of us."

MINUTES MATTER

Be considerate of other people's time when you make a phone call. It only takes a minute to ask "Is this a good time for you?"

Checkpoints

You have discovered ways to minimize emergency requests from bosses and coworkers that sap your time.

You have initiated contingency plans for personal emergencies that inevitably crop up now and then and leave your schedule in a train wreck.

You have taken steps that allow you to quickly respond to equipment failure and still keep your momentum moving forward.

You have learned to identify and avoid coworkers who interrupt your work schedule with superfluous agendas.

You have realized that how you plan or participate in meetings can have a direct impact on the time needed to spend in them.

You have evaluated your telephone habits and decided on ways in which to optimize your time spent in conversations with others.

In the next chapter, you will see how to manage your travel time.

Have Briefcase, Must Travel

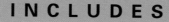

INCLUDES

- Preparing for business trips
- Traveling by air
- Renting cars
- Traveling by car
- Choosing business-friendly accommodations
- Making the most of dining alone
- Getting back into the office mode after a trip

FAST FORWARD

Plan in Advance at the Office ➤ *pp. 135–136*

- Create a portable office supply case—pens, Post-its, calculator, small stapler, and so on—and have it ready to throw into your briefcase or luggage.
- Supply your travel agent or the person who arranges your travel with a reusable set of general guidelines—preferred airline and frequent flyer numbers, hotel preferences, car rental choices, credit card numbers for billing, and so on—to save you the time of repeating this information each time a trip is booked.
- Plan your itinerary so that you can get as much accomplished on a single trip as possible, and leave printed copies of your itinerary, including phone numbers, with essential people.
- Arrange for someone at the office to monitor your voice mail and the flow of incoming work on your desk during your absence and be sure that this person is able to find needed information in your files or on your computer when you call in for updates.

Take Needed Equipment with You ➤ *p. 136*

- Decide what items—laptop, tape recorder, cellular phone—will be essential for you to complete the planned work you intend to accomplish on your trip, and have them ready to go.
- Remember to carry your organizer and calendar, along with your files to read, while on the road.

Plan in Advance at Home ➤ *p. 137*

- Determine what services you will need to take care of daily needs on the homefront while you are away—child care, pet care, taking in the mail and papers, watering plants, and so forth—and have a plan, with alternatives, that can be put into place on quick notice.

- Leave details of your itinerary with your family or a friend or neighbor in case you need to be contacted for an emergency.

Pack Efficiently ➤ *pp. 137–140*

- Limit yourself, if possible, to one piece of carry-on luggage in addition to your briefcase to minimize the time needed traveling through airports as well as time needed for packing and unpacking.
- Maintain a ready-to-go toiletry case with travel-size products in the piece of luggage you carry most often. Replenish supplies when the toiletry case is empty—not just when you're ready to take off.
- Choose outfits for your trip that can be mixed and matched and layered and that require little care after being packed. See that each can be worn with the one and only pair of shoes you pack. Your second pair will be the comfortable shoes in which you travel.

Air Travel ➤ *pp. 140–142*

- Save time by having your seat assignment and boarding pass delivered to you prior to arriving at the airport.
- Assume that delays are likely to occur. Plan for enough time between connecting flights and avoid taking the last flight of the day in case it is canceled.
- Arrive at the airport in time to check luggage (if needed), check yourself in, and be at the gate prior to the first call for boarding.
- Join an airline club, if you fly frequently, to speed the process of check-in or changing flight plans and to benefit from access to superior space and amenities for working while waiting for takeoff.

Rental Cars ➤ *pp. 142–143*

- Reserve the type of car you need for your trip in advance and know whether or not you will need to purchase additional insurance from the rental company.
- Use a rental car company that has multiple locations in the area in which you are traveling. This will insure that the car you want will be waiting for you.

Drive to Your Destination ➤ *pp. 144–146*

- Consider driving instead of flying whenever the estimated driving time is approximately the same as the combined time needed to get to and from airports, actual flight time, and time to rent a car.
- Invest in inexpensive plastic crates to organize an "office on wheels" for the backseat or trunk of your car.
- Consider using GPS (Global Positioning System) for your laptop if you travel by car frequently.
- Follow commonsense safety precautions when you decide to drive and do business at the same time.

Hotels and Lodging ➤ *pp. 146–148*

- Choose a hotel that caters to the business traveler and that is located near to where you will be conducting your business.
- Be sure that you can connect your modem so you can communicate with your office through e-mail.
- Set up a business-only area—with your work and portable supplies—when you arrive at your hotel and keep this area separate from your personal belongings and space.
- Keep track of your expenses on a daily basis while you are away.

Dining Alone ➤ *pp. 148–149*

- Refuse to be intimidated at the thought of dining alone. Instead, consider it an opportunity to relax in a pleasant environment as you treat yourself to the satisfaction of winding down after a full day.
- Take reading material with you or use the time between courses to make lists, jot notes on the day's work, or review your organizer and calendar for the next day.

When You Return to Your Office ➤ *pp. 149–150*

- Assume that the morning of your first day back will be needed for organizing the work waiting for you.
- Valutize the work that has accumulated on your desk while you were gone and dispense of the important tasks right away.
- Avoid scheduling appointments for your first day back in the office.

Whether you travel for business by rail, road, or in the air, business trips *do* take time. So, before you pick up your briefcase and head for a plane, train, bus, or car, you may want to think about the potential of saving time and money by doing business from your desk instead of on the road.

Some busy persons who've had it with too much business travel are replacing some of their out-of-town trips with such time-saving solutions as having people come to them or opting for phone calls, faxes, and e-mail, along with video- and teleconferencing. They're quick to cite the disadvantages of living in hotels, losing time getting to and from airports, waiting to board the plane, sitting on planes till take-off, and coping with delays and layovers. They say they accomplish more in the office than traveling and living in hotels.

Be that as it may, though, *some* business travel is usually a must, so a second, and advantageous, view is to look at it as such positives as coveted uninterrupted time on planes, in cars and mass transit, and in stretches of time alone in hotels.

On a plane:	You can read, plan, and catch up on your work.
In a car:	You can listen to and dictate tapes while behind the wheel and read or make phone calls when you're not driving.
On mass transit:	You can do all of these activities—as long as you do them quietly.
In hotels:	You can set up an office for work or use your time-alone hours for things for which there's no time at home—watching movies you've been wanting to see, playing computer games, or reading a book you've been waiting to read.

This chapter's streamliners take this second view. As such, they'll facilitate your time.

Though many of the clock-beater speed-ups will apply to overnight trips to conventions, training sessions, seminars, and meetings, most are also timewise for daily commutes and one-day trips.

Preparing for a Trip

At-Work Preparations

If you don't already have one, set up a personal *travel to-do* list in a file folder or on your computer. Write reminders on it as you go. You'll soon have a fairly foolproof list to help you minimize stress and maximize effectiveness prior to your trips.

Ten Basic Travel To-Dos

1. *Put together a carry-along office.*   Include notepads, pens and pencils, highlighter, calculator, scissors, Scotch tape, paper clips, Post-it notes, postcards, stamps, and a miniature stapler. Place the items in a plastic zipper pencil case which is always at the ready to slip into your briefcase (or your briefcase substitute). Large mailing envelopes obviously won't fit into your pencil case, but as part of your carry-along office, take either large mailing envelopes and/or Federal Express envelopes preaddressed to and billed to the office. This will make shipping material back to the office quick and easy.

2. *Have a travel agent (or the person in your office who handles travel) make your plans.*   Don't take your time to make them. Professional organizer Stephanie Denton tells the story of a training-specialist client who travels to many cities to speak at presentations. When she found that making travel arrangements was taking a lot of her time, Denton helped her develop a two-page master travel list which the trainer, in turn, gave to her travel agent. Now, instead of the trainer's needing to spend time on the phone with the travel agent for each trip, the travel agent takes care of everything. The master travel list includes such things as frequent flyer numbers, rental car numbers, hotels meeting rooms, and the equipment the trainer will require.

3. *Prepare and print copies of your written schedule and itinerary with phone numbers, hotels, and all the on-tap information you need for the trip for yourself and essential people at work and at home.*

4. *Set up your briefcase with separate files for the things you plan to work on while traveling.* Color coordinate the files. Include a "To Read" file, and to keep your "To Read" from being too bulky fill it with clipped-out articles you want to read—not whole publications.

5. *Make notes (with phone numbers and locations) on the key people you will see.*

6. *Confirm all appointments and meetings ahead of time.* Group appointments together and try to visit as many people as you can on one trip.

7. *Arrange with someone to get your voice mail or answering machine messages, or use an answering service to pick up your calls if that's a better solution for you.*

8. *See that a coworker understands your filing system and how to get information out of your computer.*

9. *Read up on your destination before you go, so you won't waste time orienting yourself for both work and free time when you get there.*

10. *Start a list of things you need to do when you return.* In this way, you won't have to start from scratch getting back on track.

HABITS & STRATEGIES

Whenever you obtain interesting information about areas you visit on business, file the items alphabetically in a folder labeled "Places to Go." Later, when you schedule a trip, pull out the information on the area and take it with you as something to do in downtime.

What to Take with You for Working

In research conducted by D. K. Shifflet & Associates for Courtyard by Marriott, a study of business travelers found that

58 percent take a laptop computer with them

44 percent carry cellular phones

25 percent take pagers

14 percent travel with portable fax machines and printers

Your own special needs will determine the electronics you choose to take. But a tape recorder is an asset, too, since you can use it to dictate on the road. Carry extra batteries for the equipment you plan to use.

Other items to take are as follows:

1. One all-purpose on-paper or electronic planner and calendar

2. Scribble pad

3. Carry-along office

4. To-read file

At-Home Preparations

Post a printed copy of the written schedule and itinerary you prepared for work in a conspicuous spot so everyone on the homefront will have phone numbers where you can be reached, hotels in which you'll be staying, and all other prime information should you be needed for anything. If you live alone, give a copy to a friend, relative, or neighbor.

Set timers on your lights, stop your mail and newspapers, or arrange to have them taken in. Let the police know you'll be away if you'll be gone an extended length of time, and leave the name of someone to call in emergencies.

Your standard list of whatever needs to be taken care of in your house or apartment while you're away should include the following:

• Arranging with a pet sitter or pet boarding place if you have a pet
• Lining up someone to water plants
• Seeing that snow will be shoveled, the lawn will be mowed, or the garden will be tended if you're away during those seasons

What to Take and Pack

Try to take just one piece of carry-on luggage, in addition to your over-the-shoulder briefcase or laptop/briefcase combo. A carry-on with wheels and a handle that pulls up is easy to roll through airports, and you can fit your briefcase/laptop on it if you wish. Another carry-on alternative is a garment bag with compartments that, like the carry-on with wheels, will fit in the overhead bin (if there's no room to hang it at the front of the plane).

Your carry-on luggage makes a quick getaway possible once the plane lands. You'll lose neither time nor luggage, and with careful packing you can live for a week with one carry-on. "I went on a 12-day trip to Hawaii with just one carry-on," emphasized Donna McMillan of McMillan & Company Professional Organizing.

What to Put in Your Luggage

As soon as you know you're going on a trip, open your luggage and begin putting things inside or beside it as you think of what you want to take. Expedite this by compiling a master packing list on your computer, printing it out, and placing a copy inside of your luggage. Check off items as you put them in your luggage. It's also a good idea to jot down another list of everything you've packed in case something happens and you need to make a claim. Put your name and address both inside and outside of your luggage for easy identification.

Your Ready-to-Go Toiletry Case

Always keep a ready-to-go toiletry case with small containers of the products you use inside of your luggage—*and never take this case out except to replenish it.* If you use it *only* for travel, it makes it much easier to pack quickly.

The small-size containers should hold doubles of all your cosmetic and grooming needs—makeup for women and shaving supplies for men. Both will need shampoo, toothbrush, toothpaste, and probably 10 to 15 other things. You may want to add aspirin, Band-Aids, or any over-the-counter products you use. Keep all the toiletries in a plastic bag so they won't spill on other items.

CAUTION

Use your office address rather than your home address on your luggage.

Your Clothes

Coordinate your clothes so you can pack less and still have things that go together—shirts and tops, slacks and skirts, jackets, shoes, *everything*. Stick with two or three basic colors that you can mix and match (i.e., brown and beige or black and white). Add a third bright color for accessories. Choose knits, no-iron, wrinkle-free and noncrushable fabrics, and plan layered outfits so you'll be prepared for either warm or chilly weather.

Here are basic to-takes that work for most business trips. Personalize the list to fit your needs:

3 pairs of slacks (or skirts).

3 shirts or tops.

1 jacket.

2 pairs of shoes (1 comfortable pair for traveling and another pair that will match all of your clothes).

Underwear in baggies will slip into your shoes.

1 dressy outfit for special occasions.

1 large tee shirt to double as sleepware and robe.

Flipflops for your feet.

Jeans (These are bulky to pack. If you want to have a pair with you, wear them for travel.)

HABITS & STRATEGIES

Do not put jewelry, medicines, credit cards, cash, travelers' checks, business and travel documents, keys, cameras, electronic devices, glasses or contact lens, and other valuables in your luggage. Keep them with you on your person or in your purse or briefcase. Some travelers use a fanny pack for valuables. Others choose a special pouch they can wear around their neck.

Other Things to Take

1. Adapter for overseas travel
2. Travel hair dryer
3. Travel alarm clock

4. Plastic bag for dirty laundry

5. Folding umbrella

6. Small flashlight

MINUTES MATTER

When traveling to different time zones leave digital watches that require complicated time setting at home and take an inexpensive old-fashioned watch you can set and reset easily.

Air Travel

"Obtain transportation information and keep a file labeled transportation arrangements. Make notes of car rental, hotel, and airline numbers with notes about companies you particularly like or don't like. Include a list of standing arrangements, questions to ask, and special requests you want to make—such as special diets, smoking or nonsmoking, whatever."
Stephanie Denton, professional organizer and teacher of time management techniques

In the survey of business travelers compiled by Courtyard by Marriott, air travel was their primary mode of transportation. Two-thirds get around that way.

Preliminary Planning

Here are seven preplanners:

1. Decide whether it's better to leave in the morning or the night before.

2. Plan to fly the day before or day after the holiday crowd flies, if you must travel at holiday time.

3. Think ahead to possible options in case you miss a connection. If you have to go from city to city and something happens so you miss a flight, know what your alternative would be.

4. Have your tickets before leaving for the airport.

5. Get your seat assignment and boarding pass ahead of time, too, so you can proceed directly to the boarding area.

6. Request an aisle seat for less-confining work space—and for saving time getting off the plane.

7. Avoid booking the last flight of the day. If it's canceled, you're stuck overnight.

At Airports

- Take a cab, shuttle, or limo to and from airports. This is easier and often cheaper than parking your car in the airport parking lot.
- Allow extra time for travel delays.
- Try not to arrive or depart from airports during rush hours. Your chances of traffic delays increase.
- If you have luggage to check, do it curbside so that you can proceed directly to the gate for check-in to avoid the much longer lines that are usual at the ticket purchase counters.
- Be sure to confirm the details of connecting flights when you check in for the first leg, including receipt of a boarding pass for the connection, in order to bypass the need for any further check-in for the remainder of your trip.
- Join an airline club so, when you have lengthy waiting periods or lay-overs, you can use the lounge to work on your computer, make phone calls, and send fax messages. You can also check in for your flight here to avert the longer lines at the counters or gates.
- Arrive at airports in sufficient time to be one of the first to board the plane when the gates open. Even when your row is one of the last to board, you stand a much better chance of finding more room to hang garment bags and put carry-ons in the overhead bin when you are first among your group called.
- "Use little bits of time to do small tasks while you wait for your flight," advised Stephanie Denton. "Instead of thinking 'There's not enough time to start anything because I only have twenty minutes' think 'What small thing can I complete?' "
- Keep your tickets in the same place at all times.

HABITS & STRATEGIES

Take dollars for tips and change for phones. Even though you may have a cellular phone, public phones are less expensive for some of your calls.

In the Air

This is the uninterrupted time you've been wishing for, so it's an ideal setting for taking out your briefcase files and getting to work on one. Another alternative is to settle in with your to-read file. If you don't need the clipped articles when you're finished, toss them. Don't carry them back with you.

"I can get more work done on a plane than at any other time," Debbie Gilster of Organize & Computerize told me. "Along with catching up on your reading, you can do reports on your laptop. Or, if you need to, you can sleep. I carry a sleep cushion in my briefcase."

CAUTION

Never let your briefcase and carry-on or garment bag out of your sight at an airport or other terminal.

Rental Cars

Chances are good that when your plane lands you'll head for the rental car counter. Expedite this process by choosing a car rental company that will give you priority treatment. Christy Conrad of Enterprise Rent-A-Car pinpointed the following time-saving tips when you need to rent a car.

1. Try to make a reservation with the rental car company in advance, if possible. Request your car category and price range on the phone to save you time at the rental counter.

2. Verify whether your company insurance will transfer to the rental car. Rental companies offer coverage in the event yours doesn't transfer, but you will want to find this out beforehand.

3. Check with the rental car company ahead of time if you need a specialty vehicle. Some companies have vehicles ranging from pickup trucks and sport-utility vehicles to 15-passenger vans.

4. Switch to rental car companies that have locations near the airport in cities nearby if, for some reason, the airport location where you are

begins to run out of rental cars during holidays or special events. You may have to take a cab to these locations, but this will save you the hassle of waiting to get a car later.

5. Make sure your credit card has not reached its limit when you go to rent a car. Most rental companies will take an authorization on your credit card before renting the car.

6. Learn from the rental car company any age restrictions or fees associated with your age.

7. Identify the size of the car you need. If you want seating for six, specify this when making the reservation. You don't want to find out at the rental counter that the car you reserved only has seating for five when you have six people.

8. Consider the amount of luggage you are carrying when you reserve a car. If you have golf clubs plus suitcases, you will need a car with a larger trunk and will want to let the rental car company know that.

9. Allow plenty of time to pick up the rental car. During the holidays, lines at the counter may be longer than usual. If you allow yourself extra time, you won't end up running to get to a business meeting on time.

10. Remember to have your driver's license in your wallet. Most rental car companies will not rent you a car unless you have a valid, unexpired license with you.

Two Other Rental Car Time-Savers

- Join a rental car club that keeps all of your prespecified requirements for a car and billing information on file. This gives you the advantage of being able to go directly to your reserved car without the need to stop at the rental car counter to fill out any paperwork there.
- If you have checked luggage, go to the rental car counter first and get your car. Then go and pick up your luggage. You are saving time by taking care of the paperwork involved in renting the car during the same time you would be standing around the carousel waiting for the luggage to arrive; it will probably be there when you finish at the rental counter.

Car Travel

Perhaps instead of renting a car you'll use your own for some business trips (or day-to-day work on the road). This may be highly probable because, even though air travel is the winner for getting around on business, a sizable number of people drive to their destinations.

You can save time and expenses by driving instead of flying on shorter trips by calculating the time needed for each, prior to making your plans. In order to determine how much time flying to your destination will really take, you need to add together times for the following:

- Getting from your home or office to the airport
- Waiting time at the airport prior to take-off—usually anywhere from a half hour to an hour, assuming no delays
- The actual flight time, including layovers while waiting for connecting flights
- The need to get a rental car and pick up luggage—usually another half hour
- Getting from the destination airport to your hotel or meeting location

If these combined hours are close to the same amount of hours it would take you to drive from door to door, you will save on expenses and probably stress, while having more uninterrupted time to think about your upcoming business while you drive.

Your Office on Wheels

When your car is your manner of transportation, set up an office on wheels in which, as for plane travel, you have the following:

1. One all-purpose on-paper or electronic planner and calendar
2. Scribble pad
3. Carry-along office
4. Briefcase with separate files for your work

5. Notes on people you plan to see

6. Laptop computer with modem, cellular or car phone, and tape recorder

Inexpensive plastic crates from a stationery store will keep your work and supplies organized in either your car's rear seat or trunk. Use one crate for your carry-along office and stationery and another for the work files you don't keep in your briefcase. You may want a third for materials you use on your job—say, sales samples and brochures.

If you travel by car a great deal of the time, some software to consider for your laptop computer is a product called Door-to-Door CoPilot. This software employs an advanced global positioning system (GPS), route guidance, and mapping and voice technologies. It shows you where you are, where you're going, and how to get there as it calculates the quickest route to any address nationwide. It *saves* the time of getting lost.

As previously mentioned, you can listen to and dictate tapes while behind the wheel and read or make phone calls while stuck in traffic. Some people even carry a fax.

MINUTES MATTER

After you speed up your work by using a tape recorder for dictation and other tasks, mail the tapes to your workplace so they can be transcribed in your absence.

Five Cautions

Wherever you are in your car there are five things to always remember:

1. Keep your eye on the road and *be careful* whenever you're doing business while driving.

2. Know the laws of the state in which you are traveling. Some states are placing restrictions on the use of phones while driving. The best advice is to pull over to the side of the road to make nonemergency

phone calls, particularly business calls that require your concentrated attention.

3. See that car doors are locked at all times.

4. Try to avoid rest stops and phone booths on the highway.

5. Be sure your car has been thoroughly serviced and that the tires (and a good spare) are safe.

Hotels and Lodging
Six Basics

1. Check hotels for frequent-stay discounts and corporate rates.

2. Register at the hotel nearest the airport (or your meeting place) and conduct your business from there if you have your choice of several hotels of equal quality.

3. Choose hotels that are designed with business travelers in mind. Make sure your room will include a desk or table with good lighting for your work, a modem line for your computer, and business services such as faxing and copying.

4. Try to stay in hotels with workout facilities or a pool so, for your health's sake, you can keep up with your exercising.

5. Eat breakfast in your room and put on your business attire last to avoid the risk of wrinkles and stains.

6. Find out whether the hotel will extend your check-out time if you request it the last morning. In this way, if a meeting or an appointment runs until checkout time, the extension will make your departure less stressful.

MINUTES MATTER

Hang wrinkled clothes in the bathroom while you shower. The hot water will steam them.

Working from and at Your Hotel

Nearly all business travelers feel it's important to keep up as much as possible with day-to-day activities back at work even while they're away.

The Internet is one means that frees you to do this because, with access to a computer and modem, you can get online and communicate with e-mail. Voice mail will serve you well, also, since you can leave a message on your voice mailbox that you're away but will be checking your messages and responding to them. You can change the message as you need to.

As for other work, open up your carry-along office and make phone calls, send faxes, read, prepare reports, and dictate letters. When you send the latter back to the office, some will be in the works when you return. You may even have responses.

If you're going to be away for some time, have someone check for important pieces of mail and overnight them to you. And, speaking of sending things back and forth, ship handouts and literature you accumulate from meetings back to your office while you're on the road so you won't have to carry this excess.

While living and working out of a hotel room for several days Stephanie Denton emphasizes that it's important to establish a boundary between your work and personal life to avoid burnout.

"Make a division between the physical and mental," she says. "Do what you need to do to set up one area of the room as an office. Move chairs and a desk/table, make sure the lighting is right, and have everything pertaining to work in that area. This avoids using your bed for work. Lying on your bed is for relaxing, not working. Separate the two."

To this advice Donna McMillan adds: "Make a list of the things you want to do while you're away so you don't forget anything. I block off time in my electronic organizer—client time, quiet time, play time, and phone time. If you block off your time this way, you'll do these things. If you don't, you won't."

HABITS & STRATEGIES

Tape conference meetings and workshops. Use the cue marker on your recorder and start at 000. When information you want to retain comes up, note where the cue marker is. Later you can go right to those important parts without taking time to listen to a lengthy tape.

Keeping Track of Your Expenses

To expedite this aspect of travel, minimize cash expenditures and put as much as possible on credit cards. Use one of the large mailing envelopes from your carry-along office to stay on track with your expenses by taping a company expense account sheet on the front.

As you collect receipts and relevant papers record the information on this outside expense sheet before putting the receipts and other material inside the envelope. Do this every day as soon as you get expense material so it doesn't pile up. You'll save the time it would take to fill everything out upon your return to work.

For a double check (in case your envelope gets lost), record the information on your laptop at the same time.

HABITS & STRATEGIES

Avoid being slowed down and hassled by crowds at tradeshows by not going to exhibits at peak hours. Show up when the booths you want to visit open or just before they close and plan to visit the exhibits in the sequence of their value to you.

What's for Dinner?

You'll probably have some dinner engagements while you're on the road. But, inevitably, there will be times when you're on your own and faced with calling room service or going to a restaurant alone.

While some business travelers who feel overworked at the end of the day may need or want to dine alone to catch up with themselves, others are wary about facing up to the "table for one?" situation.

Although you should *not* view yourself as a loner while in the midst of tables with couples, certain types of travelers still subscribe to this myth and *expect* to be treated like second-class diners destined for a table by the kitchen.

This viewpoint is as out of date as a turn-of-the-last-century's menu, and today a number of restaurants are instituting networking tables, corporate tables, and cluster and shared table seating reserved for traveling people who want to socialize over a meal. Ask the concierge at your hotel about such restaurants.

If you'd rather have a table for one, however, Marya Charles Alexander, editor of the newsletter *Solo Dining Savvy* offers these strategies:

1. *Take reading material to dinner.* It's a pleasure to be savored as much as a decadent dessert and is acceptable at even the finest restaurants. It also provides a great crutch if you need something to occupy your hands and mind. Letters to be written and lists to be made fall into the same category as reading.

2. *Sit where you'll have plenty to see.* Request a place by the window, a table with a panoramic view of the interior, or a seat near the door if a restaurant is known for attracting interesting people. "If you don't like a table or location offered, very nicely state what you really would prefer," Alexander advises. "Add 'I know you want me to have an enjoyable meal.' "

3. *Cultivate your server.* Reveal how much you've looked forward to the occasion and solicit his or her suggestions for making your meal a pleasure.

How Can You Save Time Getting Reorganized When You Return to Your Workplace?

If you follow the earlier suggestion to start a list of things to do when you return to your workplace, you won't need to begin from scratch getting back on track. But, still, it can be difficult to rev up your engine. You're groggy and, maybe, have jet lag. And you want to proceed in slow motion when you see the phone calls, messages, mail, and papers that may be piled up.

Be good to yourself and give yourself time to go through what's waiting for you at your desk and what you've brought home from your trip that you need to process. If you are fortunate enough to have an assistant in the office who has been "minding the store" have him or her presort and prevalutize the paperwork that has appeared during your absence. He or she can divide correspondence between external mail and internal memos and highlight those that need a quick response. Memos and correspondence can also be further sorted by project. To help you catch up quickly, ask your assistant to provide you with a brief, bulleted report of each day's office activities while you were out of town.

You'll gain time in the long run if you do the following:

- Use the first morning back to get set up again
- Try not to schedule meetings for the first day
- Get rid of unimportant things at once
- Put what's important in a folder or on your computer so you can unpack it as soon as you're back on track

MINUTES MATTER

At home, unpack immediately after a trip. The minutes it takes to do it then *means your carry-on or garment bag* won't *sit around forever waiting for you to get to it.*

Checkpoints

You have taken the time to prepack both office supplies and personal travel items so that they are ready to go whenever you need to hit the road.

You have planned for the daily needs of your home and office during your absence.

You have learned whether or not you are using your air travel time to its best advantage.

You have examined your need to join airline and car rental clubs as a time-gaining measure.

You have thought through how to determine the most cost- and time-efficient modes of travel for your trips.

You have considered the amenities that you will need in a hotel in order to maximize your time on the road.

You have resolved ways to minimize the stress of piled up work when you return to your workplace after a trip.

In the next chapter, you will see how you can gain time by working from home or choosing other flexible options.

Flex Your Time: Working from Home and Other Options

INCLUDES

- Examining the pros and cons of working from home and other nontraditional options
- Keeping work and home life separate
- Setting up a useful workspace in your home
- Managing your working and personal time when it's all under one roof
- Dealing with the presence of children in your at-home workplace
- Staying connected with colleagues and peers when you work from home
- Deciding if working from home is for you

FAST FORWARD

Discover Work-from-home Pluses ➤ *pp. 159–160*

- Take advantage of having full control over your work schedule.
- Save the time, cost, and hassle of a daily commute.
- Benefit from time saved preparing for work. It takes just a few minutes to throw on a pair of sweats and run a brush through your hair, as opposed to the time needed to prepare a polished business look.
- Increase your productivity through a focus on the job at hand without the normal day-to-day interruptions of an office environment.

Beware of Work-from-Home Pitfalls ➤ *pp. 160–162*

- Guard against friends and neighbors who find it difficult to remember that you are *working* even though you are at home.
- Discipline yourself to maintain a regular work schedule and not be tempted by at-home diversions such as doing yard work, running errands, or taking extended breaks for naps or personal pleasures such as reading or television.
- Plan for the loss of benefits that come with a full-time office job. Health insurance, retirement plans, and regular paydays are key among them.

Keep Work and Home Life Separate ➤ *p. 163*

- Set ground rules for yourself and your family concerning your working time and communicate them clearly.
- Install a separate phone line for your business needs and refrain from answering the home phone during your working hours.
- Don't overschedule your work time just because you are home and have ready access to everything. Remember to block out time for chores and household responsibilities.

Create a Productive Workspace ➤ *pp. 164–167*

- Evaluate the type of space you need for your work and establish a dedicated spot in your home for it.
- Don't let the lack of a separate room deter you from establishing a private space to work. Use bookcases or screens to divide space within a room, clearly marking off your working territory.
- Make sure your workspace is well-lighted and, noting that it is possible to furnish a home office comfortably with second-hand or repurposed furniture, ensure that your furnishings promote personal satisfaction and wellbeing while you work.
- Stock up on business supplies—paper, disks, file folders, pens and pencils, and so forth—that you will use regularly. Store them in a readily accessible area of your workspace.

Maintain a Schedule ➤ *pp. 168–169*

- Choose a work schedule that fits your needs and personality (lark or owl)—*if* your type of business doesn't require regular 9 to 5 business hours.
- Take advantage of the flexibility of at-home work, but don't abuse the control and benefits you have gained by neglecting to firmly schedule the work to be done. Begin work each day on time, according to your schedule.
- Focus on deadlines for your work—self-imposed or assigned by someone for whom you work—and schedule an appropriate amount of time to meet these targets.

Identify and Handle Distractions ➤ *p. 170*

- Keep track for one week of all the distractions that interrupt the flow of your work and categorize them by their level of disturbance to your work.

- Identify ways in which you effectively handle diversions from your work and apply these methods to other interruptions.
- Determine ways in which you can avoid unnecessary distractions in the future.
- Maintain a private time journal for 60 days to track everything you do each day and to use when valutizing your current and future business activities.

Hire-out Lesser Business and Personal Jobs ➤ pp. 170–171

- Decide whether or not a helper—a parttime secretary or a high school student after school—can handle such jobs as filing, word processing, making phone calls, and so forth, to free you for more focused time on your important projects.
- Hire help for house and yard work, errands, or meal preparation when you are under pressure to meet a deadline.

Take Breaks ➤ p. 171

- Avoid the possibility of burnout on a project because the work is always with you when you are at home.
- Schedule breaks—coffee, lunch, exercise, a conversation with a colleague or friend—just as you would if you were in the downtown office.
- "Close your office" at the end of your scheduled work time and "go home" to your personal life.

When Children Are Home ➤ pp. 172–174

- Explain to your children that they should not answer your business phone or interrupt you when you are on the phone.

- Make your children feel a part of your work when they are old enough, by involving them in tasks they can easily perform—stuffing envelopes, licking stamps, getting out supplies, and so forth.
- Consider having a child care helper for at least a portion of your scheduled work time even though you are at home.
- Take breaks in your work schedule that coincide with the arrival at home time of school-aged children.
- Investigate shared or cooperative child care arrangements with other at-home workers, especially for the summer months in which you may want to be even more flexible with your work schedule.

Stay Connected ➤ *p. 174*

- Join professional organizations in your field and interact with their programs and members.
- Use the Internet newsgroups or bulletin boards to stay in touch with colleagues and peers.
- Get out of the house on a regular basis for meals or other social visits to compare notes with people who share your working lifestyle.
- Make contact with a friend each day—a short phone call or lunch—to help maintain balance in your life.

Decide if Working from Home Is for You ➤ *p. 175*

- Take a quiz to see if you have the right temperament and business foundation to make a successful go of working at home.
- Evaluate whether or not you have the resources to target those companies that might hire you.

All over the country the old work structure in which the norm was to go *physically* to an outside workplace is losing momentum each year. Instead, the trend of working from home is moving at express-train speed.

The number of people on this fast track varies with the sources. But the latest available statistics from the Bureau of Labor estimate there are more than 18.3 million home-based businesses in the United States.

There are many reasons why working from home is becoming increasingly common. Four high-ranking ones are as follows:

- Workers are finding they save time each day when they can merge the personal and professional aspects of their lives under one roof.
- The computer revolution and today's constantly expanding information technology make it possible for people to work on their own and communicate instantly with sources and clients anywhere in the world without being in an employer's facility.
- Many companies that are restructuring and thinning their workforce find it cost-wise to have outside workers they can call on when needed.
- Workers are evaluating and reevaluating the practicality of having an alternative to the diminishing 9 to 5 market in which there's no longer built-in security in the corporate world.

Although working from home is not an option that's available to everyone, it *is* a workstyle to consider. And now that it's at an all-time high, there's never been a better time to choose the flexibility of

1. Working full- or parttime in your own business or service
2. Working as an independent contractor in which you're hired on a project-by-project freelance or consulting basis to do work that otherwise would be done in-house by employees.

3. Working as a telecommuter, in which you work from home and are connected electronically to a company's main office.

All of these work-from-home categories (and the options in the sidebar) require the *same* kind of fix on your time as discussed in previous chapters. In addition, there are special considerations detailed in this chapter.

The 11 Best List for Working from Home

When you focus on managing your work time well, the *best* of this work-style is the way it provides increased control of both your work and life. It's more relaxed than away-from-home work and, simultaneously, gives you the flexibility to work around your family life and other interests and commitments in the way that's appropriate for your habits.

CAUTION

Merging your work and home life under a single roof can be an important advantage in choosing to work from home. But the opportunity to intersperse the two can also become a major disadvantage when you don't establish boundaries between them.

Here are the 11 bests:

1. You save the sizable bite of time taken by traveling to and from work.

2. You get rid of mass-transit transportation costs.

3. You avoid tolls, parking fees, and wear and tear on your car if you commute behind the wheel.

4. You eliminate traveling in bad weather and rush-hour traffic.

5. You lower your overhead expenses by not having to rent an outside office.

6. You save money on dress-for-work clothes.

7. You also conserve dollars on cleaners' bills, lunches, and office gift collections for birthdays and other events.

8. You save the time it takes to get dressed for outside work. Jeans, sweats, and tee shirts are the quick-dress routine for many work-from-homers. (But if clients come to your home, look professional. Casual clothes such as "dress-down Friday" outfits in the 9 to 5 world will serve you well.)

9. You increase your productivity because less time is absorbed with meetings, people sticking their heads in your office to pass the time of day, and other in-office activities.

10. You distance yourself from office politics and the time and stress they involve.

11. You can set your own work schedule as long as you *stick* to a schedule and get your work done.

MINUTES MATTER

Spend your time on work that will generate the most return in income and/or sales of your product and service.

The 10 Worst List for Working from Home

Though the time you gain by working from home tips the scales in its favor, there are built-in challenges and distractions that can take you right to the top of the 10 worst list. Here are the 10 worsts:

1. People expect you to do and be *everything* simply because you're home.

2. Drop-in visitors stop for coffee breaks and "I haven't seen you for a while" greetings.

3. Your best friend is sure you don't mind picking up her son from school while she is busy elsewhere.

4. A neighbor habitually depends on you to take in his UPS parcels because he'll be at work.

5. You yourself may wrongly expect you can serve many masters.

6. You're unable to separate your work, home, and family life and maintain a clear line of demarcation.

7. You fall into the trap of procrastinating in getting started on your work when you're in an unstructured environment without supervision.

CAUTION

Avoid the puttering, too many second cups of coffee, and 15 minutes more of reading or TV that keep you from getting to productive work promptly.

8. You allow yourself to interrupt your work time too often to answer the door, putter around the kitchen, run errands, mow the lawn, wash the car, feed the dog, take a nap, read personal mail, or give in to other diversions.

9. You give up paid vacations, holidays, medical plans, and other perks that come with outside employment and generally have to take care of health insurance and retirement planning yourself.

10. Your income may be erratic with no secure weekly or regular paycheck.

MINUTES MATTER

When a neighbor knocks on your door for a friendly call, say pleasantly but firmly, "I'm really sorry we can't visit now, but I'm working on a deadline job. May I call you as soon as I'm done?"

Other Workstyle Options that Provide Flexible Time Management but Are Not Always Done Exclusively at Home

Job Sharing

In this option, two people voluntarily share the responsibilities and salary of one full-time position. One may work two days another three or vise versa.

Temporary Work

As a temp, you're in full charge of your work time. You can be available only when you choose to and how often you want to work.

Flextime

This is full-time restructured work in which you select your starting and ending time within limits set by your employer for when employees must be on the job.

Virtual Office Worker

A virtual office *is described as a* nonplace *or* office without walls. *When you're part of a virtual office team you might work at home or in a client's office, company conference room, hotel lobby, airport lounge, or front seat of your car to transcribe notes on a laptop or confirm appointments by phone.*

Part-Time Work Away from Home

Gaining time by reducing your hours usually involves the equivalent of a three-day-a-week time expenditure. This workstyle can take the form of a partial day five-day-week (say 5 four-hour days); three consecutive or alternative days; or a combination of full and partial days.

Several Small Part-Time Jobs

Some people work at more than one job on a part-time basis—and together these jobs add up to a whole. For example, a pianist and piano tuner who was once employed full-time to teach and tune pianos in a music conservatory now works on a part-time basis tuning pianos in people's homes, entertaining three nights a week at a restaurant and club, and playing on Saturdays in a department store lobby.

How to Handle the Best and the Worst—And Keep Your Work and Home Life Separate

Eight Tips for Separating Work and Home

"Make it clear you're only as interruptable as you would be at a traditional office. If they [your family] wouldn't call you at the office to let you know the cat spilled a bottle of milk, then they ought to take care of it themselves when you're working at home, as well."

Paul Edwards, coauthor of ***Working From Home***

1. Establish a firm line of demarcation between your work and home and family life. Although you want your spouse and children to know you're available when needed, train them to respect your work time.

2. Discipline yourself to concentrate on your work during the time allotted to it. Then, in after hours, refrain from letting your work intrude on your home life.

3. Determine from experience how effectively—or ineffectively—you can occasionally intersperse the professional and personal sides of your life and take your cue from that.

4. Invest in a separate business and personal phone.

5. Bypass answering your personal phone during work hours and your business phone during home hours.

6. Have a door to your workplace that you can close if at all possible.

7. Post your work schedule on your office door *and* also on the refrigerator.

8. Block out time for your nonwork tasks and home chores and restrict them to that designated time.

MINUTES MATTER

Say "no" to "Got a minute?" phone calls.

Your Home Workplace: What Do You Need?

In the corporate world, often there are rules on what you can and can't have in your workplace. But in your home, you can make the rules as long as they fill the following needs.

Need 1: A Workplace That Ideally Is Separate from Your Personal Space

The way you set up your workspace can help you save—or lose—time, since unsatisfactory environments diminish your motivation to make time work for you. To create a workplace that's satisfying for the work you do, examine the nature of your business carefully. For example, a consulting business needs one kind of space while an antiques business requires another.

As I always advise, once you evaluate the type of workplace you need, it's vital—if at all possible—to establish it as a separate area in your home, reserved exclusively for your work. Depending upon your work, it can be as small as the corner of a living room or bedroom (set off by a screen) if that's all that's available.

Another possibility is dividing a room with tall bookcases (or dividers) and making one segment the workplace. Other potentials are basements, attics, unused rooms, and garage lofts or converted garages.

HABITS & STRATEGIES

Your workplace setup will change as your business changes and grows, so examine it periodically to see what furniture needs to be moved and what equipment needs to be updated.

Keep in mind that a workplace in which people come to you will need to be less casual than one in which you work alone. Make sure it looks attractive, efficient, and professional.

Personalize your workplace. You'll enjoy working more in a spot that mirrors your individuality.

Need 2: Furnish Your Workplace for Maximum Comfort and Minimum Time-Losing Steps

To be in tune with today's ergonomics, all of your furniture should be geared to creating a well-equipped, conveniently arranged work environment. Everything should be movable and as adjustable as possible. If you find yourself getting repeated eyestrain, your lighting needs to be corrected.

Be sure you have a chair (and desk or worktable) that's the right height for you and your work. The chair should support your posture and have a firm cushion and backrest that matches the contour of your lower back. Wrist rests to help prevent carpal tunnel syndrome are a good investment if you use a computer for extended periods of time.

Among other things, you'll need file cabinets, bookcases, shelves, a large wastebasket, and air conditioner. Sometimes second-hand furniture from garage sales (or unused furniture in your own home) are good potentials for starters. Old tables disguised with the felt clothes we mentioned in an earlier chapter give you work space on top and storage space underneath if the cloths fall to the floor. In my office, red felt covers an old kitchen table which now holds my computer, disks, and radio/TV. Across the room, more red felt disguises a beat-up typewriter desk and provides space for works in progress.

Need 3: Time-Saving Equipment That Will Pay for Itself in the Hours It Saves You

Depending upon your business, here's a list of must-haves and good-to-haves. Your work will determine *which* is *which* for you. But each of these items, in its own way, enhances your time-saving options.

- Personal computer, word processor, or electronic typewriter.
- Software programs.
- Printer.
- Computer disks.
- Document holder.
- Fax machine.

HABITS & STRATEGIES

Equipment failure can be a real time-loser so read the manufacturers' directions and take every precaution you can to avoid foul-ups with computers, software, fax machines, whatever.

- Modem so you can send and receive e-mail and subscribe to an online service. (It's expected more and more that you'll be able to do this.)
- Electronic organizer, personal information manager, or contact manager if you prefer one of these devices to the self-created, on-paper planner described in earlier chapters.
- Two phone lines.
- Headset for telephone work if your work involves a great deal of time on the phone.
- Answering machine.
- Calculator.
- Tape recorder.
- Copier.
- Electrical outlets for your equipment.

HABITS & STRATEGIES

When you buy equipment begin with the minimal amount you need and upgrade as you go along. See if you have use for an item before you buy everything. You don't always need the first generation of equipment. In fact, you can sometimes buy second-hand electronic equipment. But before you spend your money, make sure you're getting a good buy by turning it on, trying some of your work on it, and seeing how it works for you.

Need 4: Supplies That You Can Find *Fast*

You save time by having the *right* supplies easily available in the *right* places so you can find them when you need them. A laundry list of what you'll probably require includes the following:

One all-purpose calendar for your work (with attached essential telephone numbers and addresses)

A supplementary Rolodex

Your scribble pad

Stationery

Printer paper

Billheads

Business cards

Pens and pencils

Eraser

Rubber stamp

Paperclips

Labels

Post-its

Memo pads

Cassette tapes

Batteries for electronic equipment

Pencil sharpener

Pencil holders

Glue

Scotch tape

Scissors

Bulletin board

File folders

Baskets

Plastic desk trays and stackable bins for organizing papers

Keep your supplies in good shape and put them away where they belong when you finish using them.

MINUTES MATTER

Save time by never leaving home to buy supplies. Have an account with a supplier who furnishes catalogs and offers delivery or mail services.

Seven Strategies for Managing Your Work Time

As a starter, review the following sections:

Making a plan for your week (Chap. 2)

Your workplace and paperwork setup (Chap. 4)

Decision making skills (Chap. 6)

Saying "no" to unnecessary requests (Chap. 6)

All of the foregoing strategies apply to working at home. In addition, implement the following procedures.

Put Yourself on a Schedule and Stick to It

Although working from home, theoretically, gives you the freedom and flexibility to work whenever you want to, it's generally best to maintain regular hours. Happily, though, you can set your hours at the time you do your best work as long as you get your work done. Unless you have a business in which people come to you, you don't need a 9 to 5 schedule if you don't like that structure. Instead you can be a morning lark or a late-night owl.

To get the most from your work time, however, do the following:

Put your schedule on paper so you know what has to be done and when it has to be done.

Discipline yourself to start work on time.

Keep on top of the musts, shoulds, and want-to-dos you listed earlier and continue valutizing and revalutizing them as you work.

Make sure your daily work-in-progress projects are well set up and easily available so you don't waste time assembling the material you need for them. Get everything together before you start to avoid jumping up and down.

Recognize that routine as well as more challenging jobs have to be done.

Establish Deadlines for Getting Work Completed

Give yourself daily and weekly deadlines so you'll keep moving ahead to your final deadlines—whether they are self-imposed deadlines or projects assigned by someone else. You'll be less stressed by deadlines if you do the following:

- Estimate your time for them accurately and monitor your progress as you work
- Allow yourself sufficient time to meet a deadline and factor in a little extra for good measure
- Retake the deadline test in Chap. 3
- Keep in touch with people who assign you deadline jobs to request any feedback you require

Start a Time Journal

A time journal can be a helpful supplement to other time management tactics, and it's private with no rules about how to keep it. As you record what you do each day, you'll see the following:

How much time you give to each activity

What you're doing right

What you're doing wrong

Where you're losing time because of yourself, other people, or the combination of both

Your journal can be a temporary measure, and once you feel you're on the right time track you may want to put it aside. But give it a 60-day trial.

At the end of that time, evaluate it to see where you've improved and what you still need to change. You'll find the time is a worthwhile investment as it helps you work through time binds and recognize the inconsequentials.

Set Up a *Distraction Check-Up Worksheet*

Even with the best-planned work time you'll run into internal and external distractions that get in the way of your musts, shoulds, and want-to-dos. For a week, write down whatever you encounter so you'll become aware of your most frequent distractions. Log in how you handled them and think through how you can minimize them in the future.

Either on your computer or on a large pad create this distraction check-up sheet and fill it in.

Distraction	What I Did About It	What Could I Do to Avoid It?
_____	_____	_____
_____	_____	_____
_____	_____	_____
_____	_____	_____
_____	_____	_____

"Learn when and how to turn down business. Some customers, conditions, or projects are such a burden they'll make you lose money and waste time." **Michael Marcus, home-based business owner of Able Communications**

Hire People for Tasks That Take Time from Your More Productive Work

As we pointed out earlier, you can't do and be *everything* when you work at home. But you can buy more time for your *primary* work—the type that yields the most dividends—by hiring someone for the *secondary* work that takes too much of your time. Some good potentials are as follow:

- A person who comes to you regularly and picks up work to do in his or her home.
- A helper who works in your home making and fielding phone calls, filing, and doing other routine work. Since collecting money owed you can sometimes be a problem, this person can also serve as a bookkeeper and make authoritative calls about overdue money.
- A word processing person who sits at your computer while you dictate rough or final drafts of correspondence, reports, proposals, and the like.
- A high school student who does errands and routine jobs for you after school.
- A house-cleaning person or service.
- A lawn service.
- A take-out meals-delivery service when you're under pressure.

Take Breaks

Because working from home is "always there or only a room away," you can become so involved you just go on and on without stopping for the regular breaks you'd take if you worked for someone else.

Avoid this nonstop working by planning a few refreshing breaks throughout the day. These breaks that you *plan* to take are entirely different from distractions and unscheduled interruptions. During two or three 15-minute breaks per day, exercise, stretch, walk, jog, cat nap, have a snack—or do whatever will give you a momentary change of pace.

Close Up Shop at the End of the Day

Opposite the enticement to dilute your work hours with too much switching back and forth between work and home is the lure to continue with unfinished business when it's time to call it a day.

It's a challenge for many home workers to *stop* working at the end of the day when there's one more thing to be done. Except for occasional periods when your workload is especially heavy, end your day without feeling any more guilty than you'd feel if you worked outside of your home.

Granted, this may be hard to do when the work stares up at you. But don't let working take *all* your hours. Say, "I've finished my day's work. Now it's my time."

Then stick to this closure and quit.

Four More To-Do Strategies for Managing Your Work Time

Do *avoid monotony by performing a variety of work tasks throughout the day.*

Do *Plan as many away from home meetings or appointments as possible on the same day so your other days will be free for uninterrupted blocks of time.*

Do *Surround yourself with music and other pleasantries.*

Do *Expect the unexpected (and the bad things that happen to good time schedules). Sometimes this requires more of your time when you're right there at home, so do what you can when these things occur and be kind to yourself for what you can't do.*

What About the Children?

A major benefit in working from home is the satisfaction it provides of having more time to be with your children. With this greater availability you can give them a larger portion of your emotional and physical energies, and you yourself don't relinquish as much of the childhood years that pass so quickly.

Smart flexibility is the order of the day when you want to adapt working from home to having more time with your children and keeping communication lines open. But as part of *smart* flexibility there are steps you need to take to make working from home with children work.

Ten Steps to Take

1. Discourage your children from interrupting you during working hours as soon as they're old enough to understand what that means. Make it clear you're working and can't be interrupted every time the spirit moves them.

2. Establish phone rules. Emphasize that your children (unless they are old enough) are *not* to answer your business phone when it rings. If they do answer your phone, train them to say "Mr. Smith's line" or "Ms. Jones' line."

3. Set up rules about interrupting you while you're on the phone. Everyone knows how children are prone to do this, so let them know this is off limits. Give them the alternative of writing what they need to say on a note and handing it to you.

4. Make important phone calls and send faxes and e-mail when children are not around.

5. Get them involved in your work, depending on their ages and capabilities. At a fairly young age, they can help sort papers, stuff envelopes, lick stamps and envelopes, and be go-fors. When appropriate, ask their advice, too. When I asked their opinion, my children came up with a title for my first children's book.

6. Realize that even though you can be available, you can't always work and care for young children at the same time. Many of us have tried to do this at one time or another, but it's not always time-efficient or effective. At least during some of your working hours it may be necessary to make some kind of child-care arrangements.

7. Consider a lift from a sitter or relative who can come to you or take care of your child in her home; a day care center or nursery school; a part-time nanny; or the possibility of rotating child care with other at-home workers who will give you days in return for the days you give them. You'll also need contingencies in the wings for the times your set-up plans fall through.

8. Save your break times during the day for when school-age children come home from school or when, without any child care help, you're in charge of small children or babies.

9. Plan ahead for the summer months. Time management becomes even more important in the summer, so if you have grade schoolers, begin early to check into available summer camp programs. Ask the school, your neighbors, and local child care providers about other

potential activities. The summer months may be an especially good time to find another home-based business person or family who would like a trade-off or cooperative child care arrangement.

10. Expect to *smart*-flex more in the summer and possibly change your schedule somewhat so you can spend time with your children. Enjoyable hours at the pool or in other activities can often be achieved by getting up an hour earlier to work or going to bed an hour later.

Stay Connected

When all of your life is under one roof, a part of good time management is to take some time to get out of the house and reach out to other people. Along with combatting the isolation of working from your home, the outside contacts that you make help build your business, too. Here are seven ways to manage this.

1. Get acquainted with persons who work in your field and make dates to talk shop and socialize with them.

2. Make one *keep-in-touch* phone call to a friend or acquaintance who's not on your list of business calls each day. This nonbusiness call may be a good time to keep the much-touted egg timer by the phone so you won't talk too long.

3. Build a support system of peers by participating in professional or trade organizations. Attend the organizations' meetings, luncheons, or dinners.

4. Schedule regular lunches or dinners with friends, associates, clients, and people who run home offices.

5. Hook up with computer bulletin boards for more contacts with persons in your field.

6. Join a network group. As you share your experiences with other members you can also obtain information that might take a great deal of your time to dig up yourself.

7. Participate in and volunteer for community activities.

Could Working from Home Be a Time-Saving Potential for You?

Take this Yes or No questionnaire to find out where you stand. Rate yourself at the end.

	Yes	No
1. *Could a different work structure help relieve the tension and time squeeze you experience in your present work situation?*	___	___
2. *Do you have the skills, interests, background, and training necessary for doing the work of your choice at home?*	___	___
3. *Do you know how to target customers, clients, and companies that use outside workers?*	___	___
4. *Are you a motivated and disciplined self-starter who can perform in an unstructured environment with no one cracking the whip as you work?*	___	___
5. *Can you get along with the lack of a support system and the camaraderie of coworkers?*	___	___
6. *Can you avoid procrastination and perfectionism gridlocks?*	___	___
7. *Are you able to estimate your work time accurately and monitor yourself as you work so you can meet deadlines?*	___	___
8. *Can you separate job demands from home and family needs and refrain from giving in to too many time-taking home chores and distractions during your working hours?*	___	___
9. *Will you know when to stop work and call it a day?*	___	___
10. *Do you believe you can stick to a time management system once you get it in place?*	___	___

Total

If your total Yes *answers outweigh the* Nos, *you have a good chance of succeeding at this fast-growing work-from-home trend. If it's an available option, the good word is* go for it!

Checkpoints

You have examined the pros and cons of working at home and considered the possibilities of making this work for you.

You have discovered ways to ensure that you can distance your home and personal life when they are both happening in close quarters.

You have found ways to create a dedicated workspace for yourself at home.

You have identified the up- and down-sides to effective time management in a home office and have developed a blueprint for scheduling your time.

You have anticipated the unique work-at-home challenge that children can introduce into your working environment and have considered ways to balance these two important aspects of your life.

You have taken steps to maintain professional relationships with colleagues and peers and interact with them regularly.

You have determined whether or not a nontraditional workstyle and workplace are right for you.

In the next chapter, you will see how to simplify your home and family life to make more time for more things that matter.

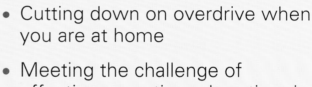

CHAPTER

10

Simplify and Equalize: Home, Family, and Nonwork Time

INCLUDES

- Cutting down on overdrive when you are at home

- Meeting the challenge of effective parenting when time is at a premium

- Setting up a daily routine at home that alleviates time crunches

FAST FORWARD

Cut Down on Overdrive ➤ *pp. 182–184*

- Update your previously made list that catalogs the things you do have time for, things you don't have time for, and things that you want to make time for.
- Create a daily, weekly, and monthly home plan that includes only the absolute necessities in terms of the musts and shoulds as well as the significant things you want to do.
- Determine how much of your time is spent on trivia and give up some of the pursuits that are not really meaningful to you.

Make Time with Your Children Meaningful ➤ *pp. 184–186*

- Choose children over chores, always.
- Create special times for the family on weekends. A regular Friday night game or video experienced together can be as rewarding as the occasional outing to the zoo. Make one-on-one time for each child, whether it's a game of catch in the backyard, a solo trip to the store, or a personal bedtime story.
- Teach your children, through example, about responsibility, initiative, and resourcefulness. Make them aware of the benefits of these attributes in effectively managing time and life.
- Include your children in the planning of schedules and choices needed to be made for each week and help them to respect the constraints on your time that your work imposes. Encourage them to see the benefits of these attributes in effectively managing time and life.
- *Every day* talk to your children and—just as importantly—*listen* to them about what is important in their lives.

Use Calendars and Lists at Home ➤ *pp. 186–187*

- Place a giant month-by-month calendar in your kitchen and record all of your family's activities and commitments on it.

- Make your refrigerator door part of an *information center* by covering it with all the things the family wants to know or remember about the week and month to come: school lunch menus, an ongoing shopping list, the weekly chore list for each family member, community and volunteer activities, details of the soccer team's upcoming fund-raiser, and so forth.

Start Your Morning Right ➤ *pp. 187–190*

- Get up an hour before the rest of your household and use that time for personal gain and fulfillment. Exercise to energize your body. Read to invigorate your mind. Meditate to nourish your soul.
- Establish morning routines that include getting children dressed, beds made, and breakfast served and cleaned up. Enforce the house rules developed to minimize fuss and procrastination in getting everyone out of the door on time for work and school.
- Organize your closets so that clothes that go together are placed together. Get rid of clothes that you rarely, if ever, wear.
- Streamline your grooming in the morning by making sure toiletries and products that you use daily are out in the open and don't have to be searched for.

Make the Transition from Work to Home Smooth ➤ *p. 190*

- Leave your office *mentally* as well as physically when you return home at the end of the day and refocus your thoughts on the evening to come.
- Give yourself some time with children before the dinner and evening activities kick into gear—a time for pleasure and renewal free from arguments, nagging, or outside interruptions.

End Your Day Positively ➤ *pp. 191–194*

- Enlist your family's help in making sure that everything needed to start your tomorrow morning off right is set up the evening before—lunches prepared, homework and books ready to go, clothes clean and laid out. Put everything possible right by the door to be grabbed easily in the morning.
- Limit outside activities during the work week to one or two nights, tops. Choose only those that will be meaningful to you.
- Enjoy the interactions of bath, story, and bedtime with your children by adhering to firm rules for them. No matter how tired you are, remember how quickly these precious parenting rituals will pass.
- Avoid letting housework and children dominate all of your evening time. Make sure that you and your spouse or mate have some quality time each evening and that one or two evenings each week you will cover for each other so that you each also have some personal time.
- Leave the day's hassles behind when you climb into bed. Be thankful for the good things that occurred and get a restful night's sleep.

The way you arrange your time off from work is another link in the mainline track to good time management since *time-off* hours are *time-on* time for the other roles in your life.

The switch to *these* hours overwhelms you at times because there's so much to do. But home, family, and nonwork pursuits are just as important in time management as your hours on the job.

The tips for the nonwork hours in this chapter and Chap. 11 deal with both men and women's time since, even though home and family was once mostly women's domain, today's men (whether they're single or a part of a couple) wrestle with the work/home balance that's so common for women.

With most couples needing two incomes, note what the genders say:

He says: "Recently I was panic-stricken as I dodged in and out of 6 P.M. traffic to pick up my son from day care. It's my responsibility to do this the three nights a week my wife works late. But I forgot what day it was when I got tied up with a project at work. By the time I remembered about my son it was time for the day care to close. I finally made it a half hour late, and my son was waiting with his teacher—but he felt he had been abandoned. I'll never forget the scared look on his face, and I'll never forget him again! But it's hard to juggle everything with a new house, a toddler, and a baby. At night my wife and I spell each other feeding and changing the baby. In the morning we're wiped out."

She says: "I have three children in three different schools and ten different sports and afterschool programs. In the morning I'm up at 5 A.M. and showered and dressed by 5:30. Next, I fix breakfast while the kids get dressed and my husband makes the beds.

While everyone eats, I eat standing up, so I can fold yesterday's laundry and empty the dishwasher from dinner to make room for breakfast dishes. Then, it's getting the kids off to school before I leave for work. I'm home from work at 3 P.M. to chauffeur the children around. I feel used up at the end of the day, and sometimes I think I work harder at home than I do at work."

Home schedules like this are de rigueur in many people's lives and, even in homes without child care, most of us feel that finding time for the following:

"We see our role at work as completely separate from our role at home, and neither as having much to do with other roles such as personal development or community service. As a result, we think in terms of 'either/or'—we can focus on either one role or another. Balance isn't either/or; it's and."
Stephen R. Covey, author of
First Things First

House chores and routines	Recreation
Family and friends	Free time
Personal interests	Hobbies
Exercise	Social life
Volunteer work	Education

can be as defeating as a jigsaw puzzle in which nothing fits into place.

But you *can* find ways to fit the essentials into the spots where you want them by using many of the time techniques you implement on your job, such as planning ahead, setting up a schedule, and valutizing what's most essential.

What you need is a workable plan that will cut down on overdrive.

This chapter lays out a plan for (1) cutting down on your overdrive, (2) meeting the challenges of time versus children, and (3) alleviating time crunches in your daily routine. In Chap. 11, you'll see how to spend (1) *less* time on humdrum but have-to-do cleaning, cooking, laundry, and errands, and (2) *more* time on the other assorted matters that are part of successful time, life, and self-management.

The Cut-Down-on-Overdrive Plan

Return momentarily to Chap. 1 and review your filled-in step-by-step lists of the things I do have time for, the things I don't have time for, and the things I really want time for. Do any necessary revisions and updating. Then, break this overall list into the following daily, weekly, and monthly musts, shoulds, and want-tos plan for your home, family, and nonwork life.

As you fill it out, confine the musts and shoulds to absolute necessities for a month's time. Simultaneously fill in some wants. Make copies of the chart and use it for both Chaps. 10 and 11.

Daily, Weekly, and Monthly Home Plan
Daily: *Tuesday*

Musts	*Shoulds*	*Want-Tos*

Weekly: *Oct. 20–27*

	Musts	*Shoulds*	*Want-Tos*

Monthly: *October*

	Musts	*Shoulds*	*Want-Tos*

As home, family, and other demands vie for your attention, this simple daily, weekly, and monthly home plan will help you manage time better—though you'll never get everything done even with the finest time management. The quest is to get the best things done.

Get Rid of Some Trivia

One way to get the best things done is to ask and answer the question, "What trivia could I give up?"

Though it's stimulating and enjoyable to engage in many pursuits, most of us find, realistically, that we *can* cut back on some lesser things (and not really miss them that much) if subtracting some of our time for them can give us time for more meaningful musts, shoulds, and wants.

Certainly not all trivial pursuits are unmeaningful. For example, a computer game or challenging crossword puzzle, which some people might label trivia, may be one of your real pleasures and *isn't* trivia for you.

Still, there's probably at least one thing that qualifies as trivia in your life. Consequently, a good first step in minimizing this is to make a trivia list of five items you can hold back on to give you found time for things you valutize more. Here's a list a research analyst made:

Trivia list

1. Excessive unnecessary phone calls

2. Sitting around deciding what to do next on weekends

3. Watching too much TV

4. Shopping for clothes I don't really need

5. Arranging and rearranging my apartment

After making her list, this analyst realized that nearly every evening, she spent about one and a half hours chatting on the phone to friends and another two hours watching TV. While she likes these pastimes, she also recognized after looking at her newly created must, should, and want home plan that she *wants* to spend more time playing the piano—an activity that she has always found enjoyable and relaxing, but which she has neglected because she didn't think she had the time. Now she realizes that if she limits her telephone chats to an hour and her daily television habit to an hour as well, she has found the time to pursue her music again.

HABITS & STRATEGIES

When you shop for clothes forego buying clothes you don't need and refrain from purchasing things that require a lot of care and upkeep. Whenever possible, buy washable things to avoid trips to the cleaners and whenever you can, shop by catalog to save the time of going to the store and standing in line to pay. Buying clothes you like and wear a lot in multiple amounts such as well-fitting tops and pants also saves shopping time.

When You Have Children

There's no doubt that having children complicates the balancing act. But, no matter how busy and time-squeezed you are, treasure your time for parenting as you watch your children grow. Cherish them for all that they are and, while you are all at the table during some evening meal, try to imagine, momentarily, what life would be like without them—even when a sibling argument, a refusal to eat spinach, or milk spilled over a clean tablemat is almost more than you can take at the end of a long working day.

Twelve Ways to Be a Good Parent in Your Time-Locked Life

"They [our children] are time-starved. If we could just put enough time back into home life to reverse that, we'd all be better off." **Arlie Hochschild, sociology professor and author of** *The Time Bind*

1. Compare weekly schedules with your partner or mate to make sure one of you is responsible and accessible for child care arrangements, the dinner hour, bedtime, bedtime talk, and backup child care when no other help is available.

2. Try to have at least one parent home with the children every week night.

3. Take the children places on some weekends. But on others stay home and play, have a special Saturday morning breakfast, watch a TV program or video as a family, and do something alone with each child to make each child feel special.

4. Remember that spending time with your family is more important than the routine drudgery of housework when it's a choice between chores and children during your limited hours at home.

5. Make sure your children learn what *responsibility* means by teaching them, through example, how to be accountable for time and actions.

6. Train them to respect your work responsibilities and the contribution your work makes toward the home and family life you share.

7. Have a short family meeting on Sunday nights to confirm who is going where and when throughout the week and who is car pooling and driving the children around. Share car pooling with other families when you can.

8. Similarly have a family night once a month. This will be different from the Sunday night planning meeting because this will deal with special interests the family can share. Start it when your children are young, since teens being teens may want no part of it.

    A possible special interest might be studying family genealogy together. Show pictures, arrange them in scrap books, and tell family stories you've heard about ancestors. End the family time with a special treat or dessert, something that's everyone's favorite.

9. Establish a *kids choice night* for meals once a week. Professional organizer Sunny Schlenger, who, as part of her consulting practice, runs

Happiness Seminars, has found it works out well to give children a chance to choose what they'd like for one night. For the other nights, make it a rule that the children are not allowed to complain about whatever is served. This is an excellent way to teach them how everyone's needs can and should be met.

10. Encourage your children to help each other rather than depend on you for everything.

11. Help with homework as necessary but refrain from making too much of your children's homework your homework. Research has shown that homework can teach a child responsibility, independence, perseverance, initiative, self-reliance, and resourcefulness. It can also teach time management, so save *your* time and help your children learn how to manage *their* time by not overdoing homework help.

12. Above all, talk to and listen to your children and, in a manner they'll understand, give them a firm foundation on principles and values.

HABITS & STRATEGIES

As part of family living always make birthdays a special event. Write the dates in red on your calendar and start planning how to celebrate a week ahead of time so everything is in order when the big day rolls around. Instead of wasting time wondering what gifts to buy for the occasion—or wandering around the stores just looking—keep a birthday list of what people want whenever you hear them mention an item.

The Daily Routine

The first step in maintaining a daily routine is a *home* calendar. In Chap. 2, we talked about the *one* all-purpose calendar—the one in your planner/organizer that (1) you use for work, and (2) you keep on your desk or with you.

An important exception to this one-calendar *advice is to have a second calendar in your house for your home, family, and nonwork doings.*

Your Calendar and Refrigerator-Door Postings

Admittedly, calendars, postings, and ongoing lists may be boring to some people. But they're beneficial time-savers—and easier on everyone, too—once they're put into place. Consequently, when you want to ease up on yourself in your home, family, and nonwork hours, give calendar and list living a try.

Your Calendar

Get a giant-size month-by-month calendar for your kitchen. A spot by the phone or on the side of the refrigerator is a good choice. At the beginning of each month record all upcoming events as they come in. Write down all of your commitments and all of your family's activities.

Include such things as work schedules, school events, field trips, tests, holidays, sports practice schedules, games, recitals, birthdays and parties, special celebrations, gifts to have ready, doctor and dentist appointments, meetings, and social life events.

Transfer what you need from your work calendar to the one in your home and put relevant phone numbers on it just as you do for your calendar at work.

Your Refrigerator Door

It doesn't matter if the door looks like a community bulletin board or classified section of a newspaper. It *works* and *saves you minutes and hours* when you plaster it with school lunch menus and other notices; school permission slips to sign; church and club monthly bulletins; instructions for new household equipment; weeknight menus for Monday through Friday; an add-to-shopping-list pad for writing down food and household items as needed; chore lists and reminders; and a daily, weekly, and monthly cleaning schedule so *everyone* can see it.

Morning Strategies

As mentioned in Chap. 1, how you get moving in the morning affects your entire day since the pace you set is the starting gun for the tempo of your subsequent hours. A poorly paced start signals frenzy while a calmer beginning shortstops those awful days we've all had in which, from beginning to end, everything goes wrong.

"Every parent should have a placard posted on the refrigerator door with these maxims: If you open it, close it. If you take it out, put it back. If you throw it down, pick it up. If you take it off, hang it up."
Elizabeth Wiegand, *The News & Observer,* Raleigh, North Carolina

Three Good Things to Do for Yourself

1. Get up an hour earlier than the rest of the household and before your *real* day begins, take care of

    (*a*) one of the responsibilities that has been hanging over your head,

    (*b*) a pleasure you want to pursue but have had no time to follow,

    (*c*) the need to fill up your spiritual fuel tank

    The benefits will be substantial, no matter how difficult it is to get yourself out of bed.

2. Exercise, if you possibly can, since morning exercise gets your blood flowing.

3. Eat a healthy breakfast, even if you have to eat yours in the car on the way to work.

CAUTION

Whenever you know there will be a variation in your A.M. routine, arrange for it in the evening instead of meeting it head-on in the morning.

Other A.M. Things to Do

Have a schedule and then add at least half an hour leeway for the unexpected—such as when you're held back by such time-losers as a child who fakes an illness (or really has one), a toddler who's determined to dawdle, or a phone call from your mother saying she has a doctor's appointment and needs you to drive her *today.*

Establish a system for getting your children dressed. Older children can dress themselves while you, your mate, or an older child can help the younger ones.

Arrange for all the adults in the house (male and female) to make their own beds. Start the children doing this as soon as they're old enough, and when they reach this age enforce a rule that they don't leave their room until they're dressed and the beds are made.

Serve simple but healthy weekday breakfasts that are easy to clean up. Have everyone rinse their own dishes and put them in the dishwasher. When people balk at first, hang in. Given time, they'll do it by rote.

See that hats, mittens, scarves, and boots are in easily accessible baskets by the door. Get an umbrella stand and have *all* umbrellas there, too. When you have a place for everything—and there's only one place to look—everyone always knows where to look.

Hang a board with hooks by the door. When people come in at the end of the day have them hang keys there to cut down on lost keys in the morning.

Keep small change for a week of school lunches that are purchased in a special envelope in the kitchen. In another envelope, keep change for tokens for tolls, buses, and parking meters.

Getting Dressed

- Streamline your grooming and dressing. When I interviewed Marilyn Miglin, a successful cosmetics manufacturer and perfume creator, she gave me the ideal guidelines: "My morning routines are so well-programmed I spend 10 minutes on my skin and body," she says. "To make dressing easier I never keep more than five sets of functional outfits in my closet each season."

MINUTES MATTER

On your busiest days, wear the clothes that are quickest and easiest to put on.

- Set up all your toiletries on a special tray in an accessible spot where you'll never have to look or dig for them.
- Put clothes you wear most frequently in the quickest-to-reach spot in closets. Group them by color or by what goes together.
- As you group your clothes, ask yourself, "When was the last time I wore this?" If your answer is "more than a year ago," give that piece of clothing or outfit to charity. Less is more when it comes to saving time.

MINUTES MATTER

Take a few minutes during the weekend to organize your work clothes for the week ahead.

After-Work Optimizers

When you walk out the door of your workplace try to unwind and free your mind from the day's tensions. That part of your day is behind you. Now a new part begins, whether your next move is to pick up children, make one or two small stops, or go directly home. If you're scheduled to pick up children, make this a *talk and listen* time rather than a *hurry up* hassle.

Arriving Home

Whether you're ready for it or not, the children who come home with you, or the ones who greet you at the door will expect your immediate attention. Plan to give it to them for a while by taking 15 minutes to decompress with them before changing your work clothes and getting dinner started.

During those 15 minutes, have a before-dinner beverage and snack and make it a pleasure time with no arguments, complaints, scoldings, or nagging. Instruct your children to respect the pleasure-time rule and, as part of it, see that they hold back from bombarding you with questions and needs before you are ready to cope.

Another good rule to live by is not to answer the phone during this transition-to-family time. An answering machine will serve you well for this after-work time, your dinner hour, and whatever time you need after dinner for family and home musts and shoulds.

Evening Tactics

Your evenings are your last stop on your trip through the day—ideally the sign at the end of the track should read "Rest and Relax."

But busy people generally find there is always more to do as you wrestle with the work/home balance and your other non-work-related roles. Here are user-friendly tips to help you with that balance.

Eight Reminders for the End of the Day

1. Avoid bringing home work with you as much as possible. If you used your time well in your workday, you've done *that* work for the day. Besides, *tomorrow* is another day!

2. Arrange everything for the morning. Specifically the following:

   —Take care of any necessary lunch preparations. If children take, rather than buy, lunches, make the lunches at night unless you've made and frozen a week's worth on weekends. When children are old enough, consider having them make their sandwiches themselves.

   —See that all knapsacks are packed and that homework, plus any other needed paperwork, is by the door through which the children leave.

   —Put everything else both you and the rest of the family need to take with you by the door, too. As previously mentioned, all hats, mittens, scarves, boots, and umbrellas should be there.

   —Lay out your children's clothes for the morning (or have them do it) so there will be no last-minute searches for clothes that aren't ready to wear. Listen to weather reports so you know what clothes will be appropriate.

   —Review who's going where and when the next day and confirm transportation arrangements if necessary.

   —Set the breakfast table and make the coffee (preferably in a coffeemaker with an A.M. timer).

"I have purchased a plastic filing case, with hanging files for each of my children. I can keep all of their incoming and outgoing paperwork here and stash the filing case under the desk near the back door."
Mary Amoroso, newspaper columnist and television host

3. Do one extra home and family job some evenings.

> —Since there are so many household tasks you *could* do at night give yourself a break and schedule just *one* necessary extra task beyond your regular routine for some of your evenings. Don't frustrate yourself by trying to do everything you think you need to do.

> —"In order to get to the extra jobs that pile up I concentrate on doing just one of those jobs each week," reports Marilyn Miglin. "If I feel my kitchen cabinets need work I do one cabinet a night for a week. If it's my bookshelves, I take another week to organize one shelf each night. But I do only one extra thing a week. If you try to do it all at once you overwhelm yourself."

4. Use discretion in taking on too many outside activities.

> —Limit your outside activities on Monday through Friday nights so you won't be running from meeting to meeting or taking on other time-consuming activities. It's usually good time management to limit your worknights' outside activities to one or two times a week.

—You may want to do some community and volunteer work since this increases your community contacts and relationships. But instead of dabbling in a lot of different things, pick one or two that mean the most to you and concentrate on them. Don't spread yourself, your energy, and your time too thin. For a change of pace, it's also smart to make your volunteer work different from your on-the-job work.

5. Have bedtime rituals for your children.

—Set a fixed hour for bedtime and stick to it—except for the occasional nights when you may want to keep children up a little later to have some extra time with them.

—Make bath time a special fun-and-play interlude, no matter how tired you are. This rite will last for just a few minutes (*and* for just a few years), so make those minutes matter.

—Allow sufficient time after the bath for a story and bedtime talk. Then end your parenting time for the day with snuggling, hugging, and I love yous.

—Turn out the light and be *firm* that this *is* lights-off time.

6. Set aside time for your spouse or mate.

—Talk about the ups and downs of your day. Listen to the same about his or hers. Discuss any important plans or concerns regarding children.

—Remember that the special relationship that you have with the one you share your life with needs regular renewal and attention to remain healthy and happy. Don't jeopardize this important part of your life by skimping on time devoted just to one another, no matter how many other time demands you each face.

7. Give yourself some time.

—Leave your calendar vacant for one or two hours a couple of nights a week to do something just for you. Don't try to catch up on anything. Simply *be* for those hours. Say, "Tonight I'm going to read my book," "Tonight I'm going to soak in the tub," "Tonight I'm going to (fill in for yourself whatever appeals to you)."

—Make your friends and contacts aware that on certain nights you don't make or take phone calls. Rely on your answering machine again.

HABITS & STRATEGIES

Expect periodic resistance to some of the musts, shoulds, and want-tos plans you make for you and for the family. Your family wouldn't be human if it didn't oppose you sometimes. Recognize the fine line between when you should stand firm on your time management and when you should bend. As the familiar saying goes, nothing is written in stone.

8. And so to bed.

—Retire half an hour after everyone else goes to bed to have still more of an end-of-the-day breather for yourself.

—Lay out your clothes and accessories, after examining them for stains, missing buttons, loose hems, and the like to eliminate unwelcome morning delays.

—When you do get in bed don't take a head full of problems and obsessions about work with you.

Finally, as we said at the start of this chapter, your *time off* from work is your *time on* for the other roles in your life. Valutize this, and take as much pride in managing your time for these hours as you do for handling your work. *That's total time management!*

Checkpoints

You have created a home plan that helps you to focus on the key musts, shoulds, and wants of your family and away-from-work time.

You have observed how establishing routines with children and including them in your planning and scheduling can enhance the rewards of parenting and diminish the stresses.

You have discovered how to save time in the morning by organizing the night before, streamlining grooming and dressing, and preparing yourself physically, mentally, and emotionally for the day ahead.

You have determined how to make your evenings productive and enjoyable, allowing time for your children, your spouse, and yourself.

In the next chapter, you will learn more about how to organize time-taking home-chore musts—and continue to have time for pleasurable shoulds and want-to-dos.

Minimize *Must* Home Chores Time, Maximize *Should, Want, and Soul-Searching* Time

- Putting the at-home *musts*—cleaning, laundry, shopping, and meal preparation—on a fast track

- Maximizing your time for the personal *shoulds*—exercise, education, recreation, and friendships

- Enhancing your life by including time for the *wants*—spiritual fulfillment and a sense of meaningfulness for all you do

FAST FORWARD

Organize Your Home for Speed Cleaning ➤ pp. 203–205

- Give up being a pack rat and eliminate clutter throughout your house: donate unused items to charity, pack away dust collectors, and make sure that all your items have a place where they live.
- Divide household chores into daily, weekly, and monthly tasks. For example, put your dirty clothes in the hamper daily, change sheets on your beds and vacuum weekly, and clean the refrigerator monthly.
- Keep all your cleaning solutions and cloths in a portable bucket ready to go to the room in which you need them.
- Don't try to do it all. Clean one area at a time. Delegate the responsibility of picking up toys to your children. Most importantly, decide that some tasks (such as alphabetizing your spice rack) are just not necessary at all.

Make Doing Laundry Quick ➤ pp. 205–206

- Give every member of your family his or her own laundry hamper, deodorize the baskets when they are empty, and return the clean clothes to them—ready for each individual to put away in his or her closet and dresser.
- Don't let laundry pile up. Put a load of whites in the washer on your way out in the morning and a load of colors when you come home in the evening.
- Teach your children how to do their own laundry as soon as they are old enough. Teens who are *very* particular about their attire should be responsible for keeping their own clothes clean and ready to wear.

Plan Easy Weekday Meals and
Once-a-Week Shopping ➤ *pp. 206–207*

- Plan your weekly menus and create a shopping list, grouping products the same way they are arranged in your favorite market's aisles. Then, *once a week,* go to the grocery store.
- Buy staple items in bulk when you can, avoiding the need for long shopping lists each week.
- Dedicate a drawer in your kitchen for all the items needed for putting together the daily lunchboxes so that they are at the ready.
- Prepare entrees in double or triple amounts and freeze the extra portions for quick reheating, accompanied by different side dishes, on busy weekday nights.
- Discover local eateries that have take-outs you enjoy—Chinese, pizza, chicken—and plan on this option one night a week.
- Set family rules about setting and clearing the table and putting dishes into the dishwasher. Sharing these chores contributes to minutes-matter time.

Shortcut Errands ➤ *pp. 207–208*

- Have a place and container set aside for collecting things you need for errands, for example, clothes for the dry cleaner, library books to return, deposit slips for the bank, shopping coupons, and an errand pad.
- Do all of your errands at one time—buying stamps at the post office, filling up the car with gas, going to the ATM. Choose locations in the same general area for these and similar errands.
- Take advantage of delivery services when you can and avoid running your other errands during rush hours.

Share the Workload ➤ *pp. 208–209*

- Create a plan for sharing the must home chores and divide the work accordingly to fit the likes, dislikes, and abilities of your household members as much as possible.
- Show and explain to others, particularly children, what needs to be done and how to do it. Then let them proceed without criticism or monitoring. Getting the job done is the key, not necessarily doing it exactly the way you might do it yourself.
- Appreciate everyone's efforts and contributions.

Everyone Should *Have Time for Exercise* ➤ *pp. 209–210*

- Incorporate exercise into your daily routine for better physical and mental health.
- Vary the types of exercise you do not only to fit your timetable but to keep you motivated as well.

Everyone Should *Have Feed-the-Brain Time* ➤ *pp. 210–211*

- Take a two-hour course on something of interest to you one evening a week or on Saturday mornings at your local community college.
- Explore the variety of television programming now available not only through PBS but on such cable channels as the Discovery Channel, A&E, or the Learning Channel in place of watching reruns of your favorite sitcom.

Everyone Should *Have Time for Fun* ➤ *p. 211*

- Keep an ongoing list of all the fun things and places that should be a part of your life: favorite restaurants, books to read, movies to see, golf and tennis games to play. Block off time to enjoy these activities.
- Plan for a weekend getaway every several months to refresh yourself and to shake off the accumulated stress of a busy work and personal life.

- Don't mix business with pleasure during the hours you have set aside strictly for leisure.

Everyone Should *Have Time* for Relationships ➤ *pp. 212–213*

- Take a quiz to see how well you do at relating to others.
- Decide to make time to listen to others, to make others feel important, to forgive and forget past misunderstandings, and to make contact with the people in your life you have neglected.

Invest Want-To-Do *Time in a Spiritual Connection—* You Can't Manage on Empty ➤ *pp. 213–216*

- Realize you can make a spiritual connection that's right for you—a core understanding of *something meaningful* that gives you strength to face your days in tandem with time spent on your musts and shoulds.
- Take time, perhaps during part of that first hour in the morning when you rise before others, to pray or meditate to connect with your values and beliefs.
- Stay in touch with the *beauty* of the world around you. If you walk for exercise, choose a route that provides opportunities to marvel at the serenity and diversity of nature.
- Listen to inspirational tapes or soothing music as you exercise or while you cook or clean.
- Make part of your feed-the-brain time simultaneously food for your soul. Choose a course or study group in philosophy or religious traditions and teachings.
- Remind yourself, daily, of the things that are most important to you in your work and life, and be thankful for all the activities of the day that have sustained these things.

From every possible aspect, subtracting time from the *must* home chores adds up to more time for the *shoulds,* and, just as importantly, provides needed hours for the essential *want-to-dos* that give meaning to your personal life.

Before we get to the latter—your *inner* management—we'll look at the *outer* management of the inevitable *musts* that, when they run on the fast track, free you to give more long-haul time to your work, family, and everything else in your time and life management.

Starting with these inevitables, this chapter moves from the lowly *must* of speed-cleaning a kitchen floor to the lofty *want* of having time to soul-search the meaning of your life—the "Who am I?" and "Why am I here?"

In today's business climate, the trend toward this *want* is a growing one, as time-starved, overworked people search for the special something that provides perspective for their busy lives.

As you start with the *musts,* there are three fundamentals that deduct time from them.

"What does it matter how much we do if what we're doing isn't what matters most?"
A. Roger Merrill, founding member of the Covey Leadership Center

1. Just as you do in your work, get over the everything-must-be-perfect syndrome. If the house isn't as ideally perfect as you'd like it, it doesn't really matter. Live with the good-enough approach and don't be stressed about it.

2. Cut down on material possessions that take time and energy to maintain. If owning and taking care of them gives you pleasure, that's great. But if you see this type of home maintenance only as a time-taking chore, think twice about overdecorating and having too many things.

3. As a similar basic for speeded-up home care, put away dust collectors and home trappings that require extra care. Unless seeing them every day means a great deal to you—and you really like caring for them—give serious consideration to stashing them away at least until you're less busy.

CAUTION

Don't add anything new to your house until you subtract an item that has outlived its usefulness.

The *Must* Home Chores

The key to handling house chores in no-time-to-lose style is to stay head of your things to-do and *never* let chores pile up.

Cleaning and Organizing Tips

Use these streamliners to speed-clean before the chores pile up.

Five Ways to Get Your House in Order for Speed-Cleaning and Organizing

"Basically, if you toss out the junk you don't need there isn't as much to clean and it's easier to find what you need."
Don Aslett, author of
Clutter's Last Stand

1. Get rid of the junk that makes your house harder to clean. Don Aslett, a cleaning expert and author of *Clutter's Last Stand,* has found that 40 percent of all housework is caused by clutter.

2. Take books and no-longer-used items to consignment stores or contribute them to charitable organizations or community fund-raisers.

3. Remove everything from each room in your house (except large pieces of furniture) once a year. Sort through everything and put back only what you need, use, and really want.

4. Label cabinets, shelves, and drawers indicating what belongs on or in each. This will make it easier for people to put things away instead of leaving them anywhere they happen to land.

5. Put attractive baskets (with tops) in every room. They're wonderful containers for the loose ends of your life that, with no other place to go, end up on tables and counters.

Twelve Tips for Cutting Cleaning Time in Half

As a major resource on how to clean, researchers at the Colgate-Palmolive Company suggest the following tips for cutting cleaning time in half.

Daily

Clear up clutter as you go.

Wipe bathroom sink after using.

Put clothes directly into the closet or clothes hamper.

Wipe down kitchen counters and appliances.

Empty trash into one bag and take out.

Weekly

Clean all surfaces in your home with one all-purpose cleaner.

Strip beds.

Vacuum.

Put an old sock on each hand and dust with both hands.

Run a hot shower before cleaning the bathroom. Wall and tile dirt come off faster when loosened by steam.

Monthly

Clean floors, refrigerator, walls, and cabinets

Recycle newspapers, magazines, and catalogs.

Ten Other Cleaning and Organizing Time-Savers

1. Hang a squeegee brush in the shower and have everyone wipe walls and the shower door before leaving the shower.

2. Wipe off faucets regularly to maintain their shine.

3. Put wastebaskets in every room.

4. Keep everything you use to clean all together in one box or pail.

5. Eliminate extra dirt from coming into the house by using mats at all entrance doorways.

6. Throw salt on the logs in your fireplace to reduce soot by up to two-thirds.

7. Tackle one area at a time instead of trying to clean the whole house at once.

8. Designate off-limits rooms for toys. It's okay to have the living room be a no-toy area.

9. Have company at least once every two months. It's a sure way to get surface cleaning done.

10. Avoid *all* unnecessary household chores that don't have to be done at the present moment if you could be using your time for higher-valutized activities. Sometimes these chores *never* need to be done so you end up with the satisfaction of not wasting time on them.

MINUTES MATTER

Comedian Phyllis Diller once compared cleaning your house while your kids are still growing to shoveling the walk before it stops snowing.

Laundry Tips

- Put a small portable wicker hamper for laundry in everyone's room. Even small children can be trained to put their own dirty clothes in the basket.
- Have scheduled times to do laundry. The now-and-then system drags on and on and becomes load after load.
- Keep all of your detergents and laundry supplies in one place by the washing machine.
- At laundry time, as you empty the baskets from each room, throw all the whites in one load. Do the colored items later while the whites are drying.
- Toss in the whites before work and do the colors after work as a quick way to keep your laundry from piling up till the weekend. Obviously, the number of days you have to do this depends on the amount of laundry you have each week.
- Spray the wicker baskets with deodorizer when they're empty. Then, when the laundry is washed and dried, put each person's things back in or on the baskets for each person to hang, fold, and put away.
- An alternative to putting things back in the baskets (if you have a separate room for laundry) is to simply stack the dried laundry on a table

and save the time of folding it and putting it away. Family members can pull out what they need as they need it, and you can grab what you require to dress small children.

- As soon as your children are old enough, teach them how to do their own laundry so your laundry time will be shortened.

CAUTION

Think about laundry time-savers when shopping. Buy only no-iron clothes and household accessories and avoid buying items that need to be hand washed.

Food Shopping, Meal Preparation, and Cleanup Tips

How often have you been shopping and heard a harried shopper say, "If only we didn't have to eat!"

You've probably thought the same yourself as you've pushed your way from aisle to aisle filling up your cart. But it's a given that we *have* to eat, so here are ways to lighten that chore.

Food Shopping

- Go to supermarkets in off hours.
- If you shop on weekends, be there when the store opens to avoid subsequent crowded lines.
- Buy in bulk whenever you can.
- Prepare a master shopping list according to the way products are arranged in the store in which you shop.
- Use the master list to make your weekly list and menus.
- Add to your weekly list any to-get items from the list on your refrigerator if the items are not standards on your master list.
- When you need to do any small food shopping over and above your weekly shopping, pick up the items on your way home from work to sidestep the need for an extra shopping trip.

MINUTES MATTER

Consider doing some of your food and household shopping by catalog to save trips to the store.

Meal Preparation and Cleanup

- Make and freeze a whole week's worth of Monday-through-Friday lunch sandwiches on Sundays.
- Have one drawer in your kitchen set up with everything you need for those lunch preparations: sandwich bags, spreaders, plastic cutlery, plastic containers, paper napkins, and single serving packages of chips and snacks.
- Scale down your idea of what makes an adequate week night dinner. Prepare favorite entrees in double or triple amounts and freeze the extras. Later, an entree can be pulled from the freezer and heated while vegetables are steaming. This system provides enough nutrients and minimizes pots and pans.
- Add to your prepared-ahead meals one eat-out night and one take-out night during the week and you're set for work night dinners.
- For the non-eat-out and take-out meals, make it a house rule that the first adult or grown child to get home sets the table and gets dinner underway.
- Clean up as you go while preparing meals.
- Put pots in the sink to soak while you're having your meal. They'll be easier to scrub or ready for the dishwasher afterward.
- When clearing the table, have everyone, including children, put their dishes in the dishwasher immediately.

Shortcuts for Errands
Seven Clock-Beating Speedups

1. Hang a large canvas tote bag on a sturdy hook and use the bag to toss in such things as library books to be returned; items to be returned or

repaired; banking to take care of (along with a batch of deposit and withdrawal slips); and lists of (*a*) clothes to go to the cleaners or laundry, (*b*) purchases to make, and (*c*) general errands to do. In this way, your errands will be bundled together in one place.

2. As much as possible, do all errands at one time so you're not constantly wasting your time running around on one or two errands.

3. Do your business with stores, banks, cleaners, and gas stations that are close together so you can make fewer stops and save the time of going from one location to another.

4. Take advantage of delivery services.

5. Use automatic teller machines instead of standing in lines at banks.

6. Try not to do errands at peak hours.

7. Similarly, avoid the heaviest traffic times in your errand area.

Above All—*Share* the Chores

There is no better strategy for saving time on the musts for family living and household chores than sharing the workload. As we have already seen, having time for yourself, your mate, and your children in the shoulds and wants in your nonworking lives depends on cooperation and each person's carrying his or her own weight as much as possible. The box on sharing the must home chores provides nine more ideas for implementing a workable plan for your household.

A Plan for Sharing the Must Home Chores Includes *Everyone*

- *Start your children early with helping with the chores. Begin with putting toys away. Then move on to making beds, setting and clearing the table, and helping put dishes in the dishwasher.*
- *Be firm about the rule that as soon as they are able, children clean up after themselves when they make a mess. As a source unknown to me once suggested so aptly, "If children are old enough to make a mess they're old enough to clean it up."*

- *Make a list of the weekly chores that need to be done and split the workload so styles fit the personalities of the people who live in your home. For example, he cooks; she sets the table and does the dishes. Or, she loves gardening; and he hates it—but he's open to running errands which she abhors.*
- *While having people do the jobs they prefer (at least as much as possible), still alternate and rotate jobs occasionally so everyone gets a crack at the most preferred jobs and so that one person is not stuck with all the undesirables.*
- *Lower your standards when other people share the workload, even if they don't do the job as well or as thoroughly as you think it should be done.*
- *Don't repeatedly tell people how to do things—including children. After you describe what's expected and train children how to do chores, stay off their backs while they're doing their share. Save your time for something else.*
- *Have an understanding that in periods of crises and nonnormal periods, you'll shoulder each other's responsibilities.*
- *Appreciate everyone's contributions and efforts.*
- *Supplement the in-house sharing the must home chores plan by hiring outside help when necessary.*

HABITS & STRATEGIES

When people share the workload, realize there's more than one way to do things. Everyone doesn't have to work in the same way.

The *Shoulds* That Matter

At the same time you minimize time for your *musts*, you should maximize time for *shoulds*, both the *shoulds* that are second cousins to *musts* and the *shoulds* that are *meant* to be *shoulds* because of the way they contribute to the best use of your time. Following are four that really matter.

Your Exercise *Shoulds*

Taking time for exercise on a daily basis makes a tremendous difference in optimizing your time because, when you are physically fit, you maintain your energy levels and function on your best mental plane. To make yourself *make* time for exercise, try the following:

- Regard it as just as important as your other commitments.
- Make it part of your routine when you set up your weekly calendar and schedule.
- Designate a specific time span for exercising. Early morning is an ideal time, if you can do it then, because the physical exertion will help activate your metabolism to a level of optimal functioning through the day. If you can't exercise then, set aside a specific time frame at another point during the day or evening.
- Give yourself different types of exercise options for variety. Then once you get into a program, assign an hour for one type (walking), 30 minutes for another (treadmill or exercise bike), and 15 minutes for calisthenics for the days you have no time.
- When you can't exercise for your longest time span, cut it down to a shorter one.

HABITS & STRATEGIES

Refuse to allow your other musts and shoulds to give you reasons not to exercise or to let exercising go by the board with "I'll do it tomorrow" when you're pressed for time.

Your Ongoing Education and Learning *Shoulds*

Additional education is one of the *shoulds* busy people say they'd like to have more time for. But where do you find a place for it in your already crowded life?

The answer is in two-hour stints that will stimulate your brain power and keep you mentally alert. In two-hour stints, you can pursue ongoing education at community colleges, university extension courses, study groups, distance learning programs, correspondence courses, seminars, workshops, lectures, television courses, and reading and self-study.

There are also museums, mentally stimulating games, and educational television programs on the Learning Channel or Public Broadcasting System. Even when you don't have two hours you can speed up your mental prowess in tiny blocks of time. Says Dr. Richard Restak, a neurologist, neuropsychiatrist, and author of *Older and Wiser: How to Maintain Peak Mental Ability for As Long As You Live:* "Five minutes of stimulation can have more influence on brain power than genetics."

HABITS & STRATEGIES

Taking time for ongoing learning is the key to continuous improvement in every area of your life. It's vital in order to stay current.

Your Fun and Free-Time *Shoulds*

This is your time for social life, hobbies, and recreation, so don't make it the caboose on your time track. If you leave it till the end of the line, there will never be time for it. The following guidelines will help you hone in on fun and free time—and if your job involves weekend work, switch these *shoulds* to your nonwork time.

Ten Guidelines for Refreshing Yourself with Leisure and Play

1. Block off space for free time and fun, no matter how limited the time has to be. It's a terrible thing to forget how to play, so keep yourself open to it.

2. Set up a fun list of things to do. Include recommended movies, videos, books, compact disks, records, tapes, and places to go. When you've seen the movie, read the book, or gone to the suggested place, cross that off the list and add new things so the list is ongoing.

3. Similarly, maintain a list of favorite restaurants on your Rolodex. Note their addresses, phone numbers, where you like to sit, and directions for getting to them.

4. Use some of your 48 hours of weekend time for free time and fun rather than treating Saturdays and Sundays as catch-up rounds of nonstop cleaning, cooking, laundry, and errands. Obviously, different

"Play is critical and essential to maintaining abundant energy because it allows the creative right hemisphere of the brain to come up with new solutions and options to situations that are tiring the orderly left hemisphere of the brain. By learning to take a few fun breaks throughout the day, you release tension, open blocked thinking, and stimulate an energy boost." **Ann McGee-Cooper, author of *You Don't Have to Go Home from Work Exhausted***

Your Reach-Out-to-People *Shoulds*

Time management at the cost of relationships is not *the time track to travel, so as you plan and schedule your time, valutize reaching out to people.*

A manager I once knew rigidly scheduled every minute from the moment he arose in the morning until he retired at night. If you cut into his schedule—say, the fifteen minutes when he played solitaire—the "drop dead" look that you received sent you scurrying on your way. In the end, the manner in which he was viewed for his no-time-for-people life was with 10 people at his funeral.

Reaching out to people in your time off from work is one of life's greatest pleasures and not *making yourself available for this is time management at its worst. To be sure you're handling this* should *well, rate yourself on this people test. Mark* A *for* usually, B *for* Sometimes, *and* C *for never.*

People Test

_____ *Do you know how to make people feel important and good about themselves?*

_____ *Do you help people over rough spots?*

_____ *Do you understand when to be open and honest about giving constructive criticism and when to abstain from any type of comment?*

_____ *Do you make at least one phone call a week to at least one person you haven't talked with for a while?*

_____ *Do you regard the care-giving role that confronts most people at one time or another as filling a need for someone you love rather than one more to-do for which you have no time?*

_____ *Do you forgive and forget when a bad situation or misunderstanding is a thing of the past?*

_____ *Do you hold back from being too judgmental?*

_____ *Do you refrain from asking for and expecting too much of other people?*

_____ *Do you listen to people?*

_____ *Do you show appreciation and say "thank you"?*

Scoring

Mostly *A* answers: *You're spending time well in relating to people.*

Primarily *B* answers: *You're doing a fairly good job, but there's room for improvement.*

Chiefly *C* answers: *You're way off track in your relationships. Find time to devote more thought, energy, and time to this.*

"To be as available as possible to others requires that we be continually aware of who we are psychologically, and where we are spiritually. In other words, we must make an effort to be as 'self-aware' as possible."
Dr. Robert J. Wicks, professor of pastoral counseling at Loyola College and author of *Availability*

weekends will have different needs depending on the circumstances. But if you've kept up with many of your home-chore tasks during the week, you won't need as much time for this nitty-gritty on weekends.

5. Select one weekend a month and set aside time for *musts* that have accumulated despite your best planning, if you absolutely have to do them. Then get them done as fast as you can so that for the rest of the weekend you can reward yourself with time for what you want to do.

6. See that your weekend pursuits provide a mental and physical change from your work week activities. Often you're more productive during the week if you've had a restful, relaxing, and change-of-pace weekend.

7. Start the weekend by doing something nice for yourself.

8. Do things with your family during the weekend, too, but when you're planning fun things for all, make sure they're fun for everyone.

9. Take a mini-vacation on a weekend if your busy life prevents a longer one at certain times.

10. Keep your mind off business. *Don't* mind the store mentally.

The Heart and Soul *Want-To-Dos*

In California, a group of executives—lawyers, human resource managers, tax accountants, and other professionals—meet weekly in their time off from work for a power meal for the soul. They're participants in The Spirituality at Work Project, a program that seeks to explore the practical connections between spirituality and work. "This ministry is . . . about helping people who are looking for deeper meaning with what they do," says Whitney Robertson, the project's director.

In New Jersey, Johanna Garaventa, with a busy career in the health field, goes to mass every morning. "I began this when I read about a young boy who, with his companion, was accosted at a shopping mall by an attacker who wanted their jeep," she says. "The attacker took them to a wooded area, made them lay face down in the snow, and shot them in the head. One boy, Michael, died and the thought of his last moments moved me to the point I decided I had to do something about society's stress and lost perspective.

"First I thought 'What can one person do?' Then I realized that one person can pray for the whole world, so I started attending mass daily to assist others by prayer. I began doing this for Michael but, as I prayed for others, I ended up receiving serenity myself. Now, no matter what happens in a day, stress does not bother me. It's amazing how much people-made stress there is in our lives—and how little God-given stress there is."

In explaining why spirituality is becoming more and more of a *want* in a stress-filled world, Dr. Jyotsna Sanzgirl, an organizational psychologist and dean at the California School of Professional Psychology, suggests that people are, first, taking another look at reasons why they come to the workplace and, second, finding that those who balance their inner and outer lives are much more productive on the job. Dr. Robert J. Wicks, professor of pastoral counseling at Loyola College and author of *Availability* and *Touching the Holy,* adds, "People are thirsting for something deep. There is a hunger for something truly meaningful."

MINUTES MATTER

Take breaks to listen to your heart and soul speak.

Time for Your Soul—You Can't Manage on Empty

Soul time and spirituality are the mainsprings of your life, the cores that provide something meaningful and the strength to face time-stressed days. Many people think that when they have more time they'll have some soul time, too. But you don't have to wait till your time is in order to make spiritual connection a part of time and life management. Here are 12 things to do.

Twelve Ways to Nurture Your Soul

1. Seek active spiritual growth by believing in and reaching out for guidance from whatever higher power conforms to your personal beliefs.

2. Simultaneously reach deep inside yourself to soul-search and solidify your values so you can stay in control of them—even in the midst of pressure.

3. Invest in the power of prayer. Pray for yourself and others and give thanks for all you've received.

4. Try regular attendance at a weekly religious service that's in accordance with your creed—Christianity, Judaism, Buddhism, Islam, whatever. This will tune up your spirit for the subsequent workweek.

5. Reinforce your spiritual beliefs by staying in touch with nature. Take walks in natural settings, in the woods, by the sea. Look out of your windows and marvel at nature's gifts. When I see the glory of the red maple tree near my home in its blaze of fall color, Robert Browning's "God's in his heaven" becomes a timeless testament of faith.

6. Value solitude and a quiet corner in your life in which you do nothing but sit and meditate. Feel at home in the stillness of your thoughts.

7. Close your eyes and listen to spiritual and inspirational music.

8. Read and listen to tapes that provide spiritual nourishment. For 15 minutes a day, read a book on philosophy, spirituality, or the great religious teachings and traditions.

9. Join a study group. A bimonthly hour with others who are searching for knowledge and meaning can lift you up and help you grow spiritually.

10. Start a spiritual journal to provide ongoing insight into spirituality's imprint on your life.

11. Develop a vision for yourself and your purpose in life. Envision what you want to be, regardless of the roadblocks that get in your way. As a teacher who got back on track after a year of derailments puts it, "Believe me, I'm not through yet."

12. Practice soul-nurturing daily to refresh and renew yourself for the multiple roles in your time and life management.

"Here is an hour . . . in which to think a mighty thought, and sing a trifling song, and look at nothing."
Edna St. Vincent Millay, American poet

HABITS & STRATEGIES

Effective ongoing time management means seeing all of your roles as the sum total of who you are. On a weekly or monthly basis be sure the parts of you include time well spent on work, home life, family, friends, spirituality, education, exercise, play, relationships, recreation, relaxation, volunteer activities, social life, and other personal interests.

Checkpoints

You have realized that you can speed through the household cleaning by removing clutter and dividing up chores into daily, weekly, and monthly musts.

You have taken steps to lessen time spent on the drudgery of laundry by involving family members in the collection and putting away of their own clothes.

You have determined ways in which you can limit grocery shopping to once a week and minimize time spent on other errands as well.

You have decided, with the input of your family, on a plan for sharing the chores that must be attended to during each day and week.

You have found ways to incorporate exercise and mental stimulation into your daily life.

You have considered what leisure activities are important to your sense of well-being and have implemented plans for devoting time to them.

You have discovered that renewing your inner self can be incorporated into many aspects of your daily life and have dedicated yourself to maintain this connection.

In the next chapter, you'll see how to season the time management tools and techniques you've learned with a quick dash of Minutes Matter tips.

12

Gain Time with Things to Do Two at a Time, Once, and In Between

INCLUDES

- Implementing tasks at work that you can do two at a time
- Consolidating tasks into two at a time away from the office
- Determining the tasks that should be done *just once*
- Making in-between times count
- Gaining extra minutes throughout your day using time-tested tips

FAST FORWARD

When You're on the Phone ➤ *p. 223*
- Have separate phone lines for your fax and modem connection so that when you are talking on the phone, you can still send and receive faxes.
- Use a headset or speaker phone so that your hands are free to sort papers or input information into your computer while you talk.
- Read e-mail or scan the newspaper, download files, or type notes into your computer while you are on hold.

When Working at Your Computer ➤ *pp. 223–224*
- Sort through the day's mail, skim reading material, and proof outgoing mail while your computer is booting up or you download files.
- Sneak in five minutes of exercise—stretching or lifting small weights—while waiting for printing to be completed.

When You're Traveling or Commuting ➤ *pp. 224–225*
- Catch up on your reading and memo writing while you commute on public transportation or travel long distance for the job.
- Listen to tapes of recent meetings and dictate thoughts into your take-along tape recorder while driving to and from work or on your way to other meetings.

When You Exercise ➤ *p. 225*
- Watch the news on television or listen to a motivational tape as you walk on the treadmill.
- Combine exercising and commuting if you can: ride a bike to work or get off public transportation at an earlier stop and walk the extra distance.

- Think about solutions to sticky problems at home or work as you jog or use your exercise bike.
- Get your exercise at the same time you spend meaningful time with your family: play a game of tag with small children or shoot some hoops with your teens.

When You Watch TV ➤ pp. 226–227

- Assemble a basket filled with little chores—buttons to be sewn on shirts, coupons to be sorted, short notes to be written—and do these things while watching your favorite shows.
- Organize your monthly bills, write checks, and reconcile your checkbook.
- Browse through catalogs and fill in order forms for time-saving shopping.

Establish a Do-It-Once System ➤ pp. 227–231

- Learn what you need to know about new equipment or new office procedures up front to save time asking questions or educating yourself later.
- Perform a postmortem at the end of a project. Record what went well and what didn't and use the evaluation to help plan the structure for similar projects in the future.
- Keep your calendar up to date by filling in deadlines and meetings as soon as they are scheduled.
- Write routine memos and letters only once. Don't waste time on multiple drafts.
- Use a financial program or create your own log for all income, taxes, and bills. Put the data in once as you receive it.
- Keep your computer address book of e-mail and fax addresses current by entering in new numbers and names as they cross your desk.
- Respond to your mail immediately as much as possible.

- Maintain a file with directions to businesses, restaurants and hotels, friends' or colleagues' offices or homes, or frequently visited cities on your computer and simply print them out as needed.
- Keep an ongoing list of contacts you make, with phone numbers and addresses if possible, even if a person doesn't seem to fit into your current plans or needs. You never know when you will want to expand your network.
- Purchase gifts and cards on one big gift-and-card shopping trip. Wrap them and have them ready to deliver or mail at appropriate times.

In-between Times that Count ➤ pp. 231–232

- Remember that 15 minutes *is* 15 minutes. Don't fall into the trap of thinking that you don't have time to do anything.
- Update or make a new list, straighten your desk, check your voice or e-mail, or put away files in the found minutes between meetings or conference calls.
- Take a break to restore your energy—get a fresh cup of coffee, walk around the office, or go outside for a few minutes of fresh air.

Time-Tested Tips for Gaining Extra Minutes ➤ pp. 233–235

- Dress only once a day. Plan in advance an outfit that will take you through all of the activities scheduled.
- Put things in their place right away—dry cleaning, groceries, books and papers, and other purchases when you come in the door. Hang up jackets and clothes or throw them into the hamper when you take them off.
- Coordinate the time you volunteer at your child's school with drop-off or pickup times to avoid making extra trips.

- Do small household chores such as sweeping the kitchen floor, straightening cushions on the sofa, taking care of laundry while your pasta water is coming to a boil or your chicken is baking.
- Keep a canvas bag next to your reading chair and put magazines and daily papers into it when you finish with them. This makes it quick and easy to consolidate them for recycling.

The clock is still ticking and the minutes still fly. But, instead of missing the time train, you're now on the track to your major destination: repowered time management.

Along the way you've followed green lights for getting your time act together. Now that you're on the last lap, a final stretch of minigreen lights will give you directional signals for using small segments of time every day to make your minutes matter.

Throughout the day many minutes are wasted. But 10 or 15 here and there add up to a sizable number a year. And when it's your habit to use them well, you do twice as much in the same amount of time.

The proven suggestions in the categories that follow come from various busy people. Many are tips you'll use for work and other activities, but some are specifics for your home and your away-from-work hours. For a roundup of the latter, not covered elsewhere in the chapter, refer to the section "Extra Tips for Home and Away-from-Work Hours" at the end of the chapter.

A large portion of the general tips are multiapplicable, so, though they appear in one category, they can also be used for another. These general tips are listed just once to avoid repetition. However, for reinforcement, some earlier tips are cited here, too. Because of their importance they can't be repeated enough.

Work Tasks to Do Two at a Time

Because time is at such a premium, most of us need to do two things at once, and for today's generation that received good grades while doing homework *and* watching TV or listening to rock music, two things at once is an easy routine.

Generally, it's wiser, however, to give big tasks that require a great deal of thought a one-at-a-time focus. But there are lots of small tasks needing only minimal attention that can be done two at a time. Many can be paired with waiting time such as standing in lines or sitting in doctors' waiting rooms. The important thing is to know the difference between what you can and can't do in tandem. Here are suggested things people *can* and *do* do.

Phone Two-at-a-Timers

Ideally, have two phone lines so you can use one for calls and the other for e-mail, faxing, and sending and receiving online material. Long phone cords are a good idea because you can walk around the room while you talk. A headset can also make it easier to do two things at once since your hands are free. For instance, with your hands free you can save transcribing time by typing information into your computer while talking. During waiting or on-hold time you can accomplish the following:

- *Scan* the newspaper
- *Chop* away at cleaning out your Rolodex
- *Pull* files from a file drawer or replace files you've taken out
- *Put* new filing straight into your file drawer instead of a to-be-filed tray
- *Read* e-mail and forum messages
- *Clean* out e-mail and forum bins
- *Download* computer files
- *Delete* extraneous files from your hard drive
- *Type* brief memos and notes into your computer

HABITS & STRATEGIES

Lighten up and keep your sense of humor alive. Time management is not a grim preoccupation.

Computer Two-at-a-Timers

While booting, downloading, backing up or printing, you can

- *Glance* at the day's mail. Throw all unwanted and junk mail in the wastebasket.
- *Attach* your business cards with a brief comment to respond to mail or forms that can be returned to the sender with a short-short answer.
- *Fill* in forms.
- *Skim* reading material.
- *Proofread* letters and proposals.

- *Record* on your tape recorder bits and pieces of what would be a long phone call or letter to a colleague. When the bits and pieces add up to a whole, send the cassette to the colleague and ask him or her to respond by recording on the other side.
- *Lift* small weights to slip in some exercise.
- *Open* new office supplies and set them up for use. For instance, stagger file folders when you open a new box. This saves the time of digging through the box later looking for the folder with the correctly positioned label tab.

Three Other Everyday Two-at-a-Timers

In addition to phone and computer double-ups, here are more time-gaining work- and non-work-related twosomes.

Travel and Commute Time

- Always have with you (as suggested in a earlier chapters) your briefcase or carry-along bag, organized with such things as material to read; notes, memos, and letters to write; and cards to send. Carry scissors, stamps, a small stapler, paper clips, a highlighter, pens, a small pad, envelopes, and Post-its. Use this desk away from your desk on the road.
- While traveling home from a meeting by car, plane, or other public transportation, listen to the tape you've made of the meeting. On public transportation you can use ear plugs.
- Use your tape recorder for listening to tapes as well as for dictating, brainstorming, and recording your thoughts.

MINUTES MATTER

Pack your briefcase and work out of it for a week before a trip. You'll discover what you really need to take, and when it's time for the trip, you can pick up your briefcase and go.

- When stuck in traffic, make calls on your cellular phone when traffic stands still.
- Do minute tasks that need no thought while waiting for your gas tank to be filled, being held up at long traffic lights, and sitting in drive-through lines.

MINUTES MATTER

If you travel, combine waiting time with returning phone calls from the airport. It's the ultimate way to keep phone calls short.

Exercise Time—Match the Tip to the Type

- Turn on the radio or TV and hear the news.
- Listen to books on tape or motivational or educational tapes.
- Read while riding an exercise bike.
- Talk on a speaker phone while on the treadmill.
- Meditate while jogging or walking.
- Think through problems and solutions, for example, practice how you'll handle a sticky phone call.
- Park a distance away from your job or get off public transportation before your stop. Walk the rest of the way to combine exercise with your commute time.
- Consider bicycling back and forth to work and errands, if possible.
- Combine exercise and family time by participating in a sport everyone enjoys.

HABITS & STRATEGIES

Accept your time limitations and shortcomings without becoming frustrated and angry with yourself. Even the experts aren't perfect all the time, so refuse to get discouraged while trying to improve. The more you try the better off you'll be.

CAUTION

Keep yourself open to unscheduled and spontaneous happenings. Sometimes they're the best times of all.

TV Time

- Set up a basket similar to the briefcase or carry-along you organized with items for small work tasks. Add notepaper, a miniaddress book, needles, thread, buttons, store coupons, and a small hobby you're working on. Have it handy during TV watching.
- Buy 100 envelopes and a roll of 100 stamps or 100 postpaid envelopes from the post office. Rubber stamp your address or attach a printed label. When you need to send out mail, the envelopes will be ready.
- Wrap gifts and packages.
- Do catalog shopping and ordering.
- Organize family documents, letters, and photographs, and put them in plastic see-through boxes.
- Straighten up the TV room.
- Read newspapers, magazines, and reports more thoroughly than when you skim them while on the phone, by the computer, exercising, or pulling a quick read from your briefcase. This time, while you're settled in, use a highlighting pen to mark what you want to clip and save. Once a week, cut out and sort the clippings and put the information from them on your computer or in your paper file so you'll know where to find it when you need it.
- Pay bills. Here are alternative ways three busy people suggest. *All* can be done in front of TV.

  Alternative 1: Take care of bills and write checks as soon as they come in instead of putting them away and then getting them out again when you have to pay them.

  Alternative 2: Don't even open bills when they come in. Stick them in a bill box. Twice a month open all of them and pay what's due.

Alternative 3: Open the bills when they arrive, but don't put them back into the envelope. Instead, unfold the bill, staple it to the return envelope with the bill on top, and highlight the due date. Stamp the return envelope, add your return address, and put it into your bill-paying system till it's time to pay it. Discard the commercial inserts and the outer envelope.

In addition to paying your bills, you can take care of your other finances and reconcile your checkbook and monthly bank statement during your TV time.

HABITS & STRATEGIES

In good time management there's never just one way to do things, so put you into the rules. Try more than one strategy to find what works best for you.

Six Things-To-Do-Once Time Gainers

There are many things to do *just once* to save yourself hours of time. Here are six favorites.

Establish a Workable Do-It-Once System

- Date everything when you do it so you don't have to look back later to see when it was done.
- Write up-to-date instructions for frequently used processes or procedures to avoid time-wasting questions and answers.
- Take time to learn how to use all the features you need on new equipment.
- Prepare a memo to yourself for future reference whenever you complete a difficult task that you know is going to reoccur. Record what you did right and what you did wrong, what was beneficial and what was less than worthwhile.
- Jot down due dates for projects on your calendar as soon as you know them so you don't have to look them up again.

- Confine yourself to one rough outline or version, one edit, and one final write-up when you're writing reports or other material. If you can't get it done with this *once* treatment, you're not working effectively.
- Write routine internal memos once. Take the flak for a spelling or punctuation error and save rewriting time.

CAUTION

Know when working on a project once is enough. After a certain amount of time you're not apt to improve it. More likely, you'll simply make it different— and not always a better different.

Devise Computer One-Timers

- Use a scanner to put large amounts of printed material into your computer. After one scanning it will be there for quick reference.
- Implement an accounting program and log all income and outgoing finances just once. At tax time you'll have complete data and won't have to go through it again.
- Save every important piece of work you create on your computer every few pages while working on it. As soon as you finish, save it again so you'll never have to recreate it. Back it up immediately.

HABITS & STRATEGIES

Think about two computers if your work demands many booted-up hours. A small business owner doubles up this way with one computer to do such things as check and respond to e-mail and surf the net and a second to run business software and keep in contact with clients and customers.

- Before you take apart any configuration on your computer (or other office technology), wrap a small mailing label around each end of the wiring. With a pen, mark clearly what the wire connects to.

- Enter all e-mail and fax numbers you use frequently into your computer address book.

Use the Handle-Once Rule for Mail Whenever You Can

- Give mail you may have glanced at while at the computer a more thorough reading as required, and try to deal with anything that needs an immediate response at once. When mail doesn't need a response right away, put in it in an in-mail bin and place the bin *behind* you so it doesn't tug at you for attention. Once a month clean out that bin. If someone hasn't called you about the contents of any of that mail within 30 days, chances are good the mail may not need a response.
- Create personal-sounding form letters for as much standard mail as you can. After you do them once, they'll save you the time of writing original replies to routine correspondence.

Initiate a Directions File

- Start a directions file. Write down the directions to people's offices, homes, restaurants, hotels, and the like the first time you get them. Then file them in your directions file to avoid wasting time asking for and writing them down again. (Runner-up alternatives are to put directions on your computer or write them on the back of the Rolodex cards for people and places.)
- When you need directions to a meeting place (where you'll be going almost at once), write them on a Post-it and stick that to your calendar. Later, put the directions in your directions file.
- Write a sheet of directions to your workplace or home (along with your phone number). Make copies to send or hand out to people.

Use whatever you work on in more than one way when you can. Be creative about recycling unused material from one project as an idea, spin-off, or starting point for another.

Keep a People Contact List

- Make a notation of people's names every time you meet individuals who could be significant to your business or personal life. Fill a notebook with these contacts and their names and addresses. Ultimately you'll have an index of hundreds of names. Checking through this index is faster than going through business cards.
- Compile a list of all the phone numbers you use often (family, friends, doctors, dentists, service people, airlines, hotels, and so forth) and print it out in small type for a card to keep by your telephone. When anything changes, make the changes on the computer and print out a new card.
- Highlight phone numbers you use infrequently the first time you look them up in the telephone directory so you can find them easily when you need them again.

HABITS & STRATEGIES

When you have a few minutes, print out several envelopes to people you should write to often (such as your mother) so that when you get the next segment of time you can toss letters, clips, and so forth into the envelope.

Have Cards and Gifts at the Ready

- Buy gifts in bulk in one gift-buying spree when you see the right thing for the right person. Keep them wrapped in a gift closet so you're not in a panic when birthdays or unexpected gift times arrive.

- Purchase birthday, anniversary, get-well, and sympathy cards in bulk, too.
- Write the names of the people to whom you want to send cards and the date to send them in pencil at the bottom right hand corner of the envelope. Stamp them and put on your return address. They'll be ready to address and mail when you're ready.
- When you know a friend will be in the hospital for an extended time (or when your children go to camp), fix a whole bunch of appropriate cards, address and stamp them all at one time, and mail them out every few days.
- Prepare a master list of names and addresses for holiday cards to update and reuse year after year.

Things to Do in In-between Times

With a little here and a little there, you don't get *everything* done. But you do get *something* done. When you have now-and-then minutes between the major activities of the day, think, "I have 15 minutes" instead of, "There's not enough time to start anything."

HABITS & STRATEGIES

Use in-between times to put back into your inner life the spiritual renewal and refreshment you need to offset the stress and time pressures your day-by-day work takes from it.

Here are in-between things people report they do in bits-and-pieces time. At the end of this list add your own ideas of what you could do in 15 minutes. Some of the tasks in previous categories can also be in-betweens.

- Write one of the notes, memos, and letters-to-write that you carry in your briefcase or carry-along bag.
- Look over some of the reading material in the carry-along.
- Straighten your desk.

HABITS & STRATEGIES

Follow the example of a salesperson whose van became such a home base for clutter he never had time to clean it out until he found his solution in in-between time. Now, nights and weekends when he comes home, he parks the van by the kitchen door and, whenever he has 15 minutes, he clears out any clutter he accumulated that day.

Assemble all the equipment you'll need for a job once before you begin. Place it where it will be handy during the job. Put it away afterward.

- Make lists.
- Record expenses.
- Do an invoice.
- Relax with tea or coffee while you make a phone call to a friend.
- Call a customer or client. Often business will go to someone who just happens to call at the right time.
- Check your voice mail and e-mail.
- Send your faxes.
- Put out-of-place things away.
- Clean out your wallet or purse.
- Add three of your own ideas for what you could do in 15 minutes:

_____

_____

_____

CAUTION

File while on the phone or during in-between times. But be careful how much you file. Research shows a tremendous amount of filed information is never looked at again.

Extra Tips for Home and Away-from-Work Hours

Two at a Time, Once, and In-between Time

1. Eat breakfast while you dress.

2. Dress just once a day for whatever is ahead, unless you're working out or doing heavy cleaning or gardening. A chef's apron or coverall will protect your clothes for small household tasks.

3. Get undressed standing by your closet and hang your clothes up as you take them off.

4. Have a used clothing bin in your closet and put things to give away in the bin immediately rather than hanging them up to take care of later.

5. Pack your car once with the things you need every day so you won't have to pack and repack it on a daily basis.

6. Do your volunteer work at your child's school (for example, as a teacher's assistant) at the same time you drop the child off to save making two trips.

7. Write letters, cut coupons, make grocery lists, and go through catalogs while waiting in the car to pick up children or family members.

8. Put things where they belong at once when you come into the house with an armload of items. Dropping them anywhere will take more putting-away time later.

9. Move around the house to do laundry, unpack groceries, set the table, unload and load the dishwasher, clean up the kitchen, clear out and organize the refrigerator (one shelf and bin at a time), and cook while talking on a cordless phone.

Optimists handle time better than pessimists.

HABITS & STRATEGIES

Take a cue from a journalist who purchases a good supply of poster board, colored pens and pencils, tape, paste, and scissors for her children's school projects just once a year. She hides the supplies until the kids need something for a project so they can't use them for anything else.

10. Have both the washer and dryer going while you vacuum.

11. Pay for groceries and other items with a credit card that gives you frequent flyer miles. Then pay off the purchases each month. By not taking time to write checks or pay cash you get double value in both time and money savings.

12. Do your meat shopping all at one time when it's on sale. Buy large quantities, then break the portions down into smaller meal-sized portions and freeze individually.

MINUTES MATTER

Have a quick lunch. Then retreat for 15 minutes to a park, church, or library for some quiet moments to revitalize yourself for the rest of your day.

13. Prepare a freezer guide to attach to the side of your refrigerator or freezer. Keep an ongoing list of what's inside so you won't have to hunt through the contents.

14. Place everything together in the flat sheet after you launder a set of sheets. This will facilitate bed-making time.

15. Plug in a Dustbuster in the most convenient spot in your home and use it for five or ten minutes of cleaning.

16. Water plants one or two at a time when you have five minutes with nothing to do.

17. Make all your moves do double duty. Leave items that belong upstairs at the bottom of the staircase to take when you go up. Do vice versa from upstairs to down.

HABITS & STRATEGIES

When you finish a must *task, reward yourself by doing a small* should *or* want-to-do *task that you will enjoy and can do quickly.*

18. When loading the dishwasher, designate one slot for spoons, one for forks, one for knives, and one for miscellaneous. Put-away time will be quicker.

19. Buy a good set of knives *once.* Take care of them and keep them sharpened.

20. Keep a canvas bag near your seat when you read magazines or other publications. As soon as you finish with each, put it in the bag. When the bag gets full, add the publications to your recycling container.

Now that you're at full throttle for your time, life, and self-management, remember—always—that you need a *life* as well as a daily timetable. In the midst of all of your busyness, take scattered minutes in your days to *be,* enjoy, daydream, and do nothing. Belong to the minute that you're in—whatever that minute is.

In every way, make minutes matter. That's what time management is.

HABITS & STRATEGIES

Ask yourself every six months
"What do I value?"
"What really matters?"
"What am I doing about it—and how well am I doing?"

Checkpoints

Throughout this book you have learned how to make time management easier by zeroing in on time-saving skills and minute-savers that whittle your work down to a doable size.

You have seen how to reduce time stress and make life less harried and hurried.

You have discovered ways to get your work done and still have time left over for the rest of your life.

You have replaced unproductive old habits with new increased productivity.

You have taken daily, weekly, and monthly strides to succeed with the musts, shoulds, and want-to-dos that valutize and improve the quality of your life.

You have matched time management fundamentals to your personal no-time-to-lose approach. *Now keep going with the start you've made! It will pay you for the rest of your life!*

Thank You

Many thanks to the following people who, in addition to the author's tips, contributed their proven and most-used tips for this chapter: Mary Amoroso, Kevin Berchelmann, Wolf Braun, Elizabeth M. Bull, Marian Calabro, Carl Carter, Margaret Coffin, Paulette Cooper, Deborah Davis, Ric Day, Denise E., David Earl, Joe Ely, Fred Ennis, Mark L. Fuerst, Bill Gary, Mike Girardo, Toni Goldfarb, Charlene Horn, Jann Jasper, Emily Johnston, Ann S. Kaplan, Pamela S. Kramer, Carol Krenz, Cal Lamoreaux, Kathryn Lance, Brian Lawrence, Dorothy Lehmkuhl, Susan Lewis, Charlotte Libov, Judy Madnick, Pat McNees, Michael N. Marcus, Joe Park, Bernadette M. Pawlik, Susan Lynn Peterson, Marilyn Lynn Pribus, Joan Price, Shauna Roberts, Bob Rosenbaum, Jim Saeltzler, Dodi Schultz, Julie Signore, Linda Stern, Amy E. Stone, Douglas Tatelman, Jackie S. Tiani, Martie Tyler, GraceAnn Walden, Russell Wild, Eileen Winrock, Steve Wood, and Tom Yates.

Index